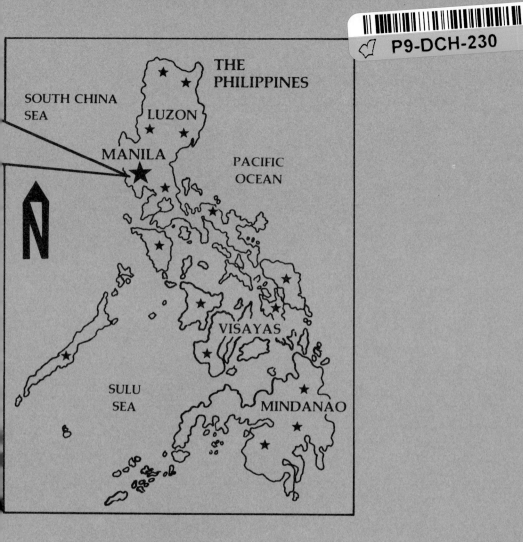

Map of the important landmarks of
the four-day revolution in the
Philippines. The stars in the Philippine map show the places where
simultaneous mutiny by Reformist
officers had occurred after the
Enrile-Ramos breakaway.

BREAKAWAY

THE INSIDE STORY OF THE FOUR-DAY
REVOLUTION IN THE PHILIPPINES
FEBRUARY 22-25, 1986

CECILIO T. ARILLO

PUBLISHER:
CTA & ASSOCIATES
ROOM 206, J & L BUILDING
251-257 EPIFANIO DE LOS SANTOS AVENUE
GREENHILLS, MANDALUYONG, METRO MANILA
PHILIPPINES

U.S. LIBRARY OF CONGRESS CATALOGING IN PUBLICATION DATA
ARILLO, CECILIO T.
BREAKAWAY

ISBN 971-91037-0-1

SECOND PRINTING
SEPTEMBER 1986

COVER DESIGN BY WAYNE LIM

PRINTED BY
KYODO PRINTING CO., INC.
MANILA, PHILIPPINES

To my children,
for their courage, prayers and
understanding . . .

ACKNOWLEDGEMENTS

The author is deeply indebted to fellow journalists Johnny F. Villasanta, Max Ramos and Ric M. Baliao of the Institute of Defense Studies, a private research fraternity, and Willy Baun of the *Economic Monitor*, for their assistance, and especially to editor-columnist Julie Yap Daza of the *Philippine Tribune* for reviewing the manuscript. The author is also indebted to Rose Natividad and Mon Mawo for their suggestions.

Credit for the photographs are due to Messrs. Johnny Villena of the *Daily Inquirer*, Mon Santos of *Malaya*, Louie Perez of *Manila Bulletin*, Pete Reyes of the *Manila Chronicle* and Perfecto Camero of the *Philippine Tribune*.

Special thanks to Jun Servano for his work on background materials and to his wife Tessie for secretarial work on the initial manuscript. The same goes to Ms. Nena Gustilo who did the final manuscript in my computer and to Lt. Col. Ariston de los Reyes, a Reformist officer at GHQ Joint Operations Center, whose assistance in sorting out classified and declassified information, has been invaluable during the research stage.

PREFACE

This book contains the official records of the Feb. 22-25, 1986 revolution and other pertinent data, including classified materials, personal files of the key participants from both sides of the conflict and analysis of a brilliant military strategy adopted by the rebel forces that toppled a repressive and extravagant regime without bloodshed. It was a classic example of the teaching of Sun Tzu, the great war strategist: "To subdue the enemy without fighting is the acme of skill." The book does not pretend to be the complete history of the revolution but a detailed retelling of events before, during and after the revolution that marked the decline and fall of President Ferdinand E. Marcos. I may have been biased when I set out to write the story because I was a participant in the revolution on the rebel side, but great care has been taken to balance the narration and exposition of events with the conscientious eye of a reporter with nothing in mind but the truth.

The first four chapters provide a cohesive documentary-drama of the revolution and the facts are fortified with unpublished data from inside the Malacañang Palace, members of the security force of Marcos, his favorite generals and key officers and advisers who had been with him when the revolution began but later abandoned him and exposed him in all his nakedness, a leader with no followers, a strongman without an armed forces to enforce his will and a loser whose only escape was flight from the wrath of his own people. The flight of Marcos was one of indecision, fear, panic and then haste. The succeeding chapters provide the explanation on the circumstances that generated the revolution, the crucial issues that divided the personalities involved, the socio-economic and political conditions that spawned the crying need for change and the collective will and spiritual force of the Filipino people known as "people power" that captured the imagination of the outside world and inspired me to write this book.

What happened in Metro Manila, the heart of the revolution, was almost equally duplicated, although lesser in intensity, in different intervals of time, in various parts of the country. Many of the details of what happened in other parts of the country were in the classified reports and reading of those materials was authorized in writing by Defense Minister Juan Ponce Enrile and done under a controlled environment to make sure that their strategic value is preserved and is not compromised.

A deeper insight into the tremendous influence of the Reformist Movement in the armed forces that moved almost the entire military organization to the rebel side is accorded in a separate chapter. It has been a privilege to be counted as one of them.

CONTENTS

CHAPTER I

DAY 1

February 22, 1986

*There is one thing that is stronger
than all the armies of the world, and
that is an idea whose time has come.*

— Victor Hugo

"WE HAVE ALREADY BROKEN THE SHELL OF THE EGG."

February 22, 1986. The time: 6:30 p.m. The place: the Social Hall on the third floor of the Ministry of National Defense building in Quezon City.

Minister of National Defense Juan Ponce Enrile and Lt. General Fidel V. Ramos, vice chief of staff of the Armed Forces of the Philippines, announce to the nation and to the world that they are withdrawing their support from President Ferdinand E. Marcos.

The announcement is the first shot in a practically bloodless revolution that is to take place in four days in a manner never before seen elsewhere in the world.

The announcement is a complete surprise to Marcos. Not until 10:30 p.m. does he make public on television the impact of the breakaway, and only to say, "I feel sad. I did not know Enrile and Ramos could reach this height of treason and rebellion."

Treason? Rebellion? How could it be said of these two men whose powers had over a decade been clipped, little by little, by Marcos, his wife, Imelda, and General Fabian C. Ver, his ever-loyal armed forces chief of staff? As Enrile was to tell a press conference hours after his defection, "They are putting people in the military command without consultation with me or with General Ramos. This is no longer a Ministry of National Defense. It's simply a decoration. We are deodorants, without anything else to do."

Treason? But wasn't it Marcos who needed Enrile and Ramos to give his government credibility? In July, 1983, the three had a heart-to-heart talk at Malacañang, after which Enrile and Ramos offered to resign. Marcos soothed and admonished them: "We have started this together; let's finish it together."

Rebellion? Maybe, because when Enrile and Ramos decided they would have nothing more to do with the regime, Marcos was hit in the heart, and as far as he was concerned, it was a rebellion. In the eyes of Enrile and Ramos, it was the beginning of a revolution that was the only way to force Marcos to step down from the presidency.

★ ★ ★

Saturday, February 22, was a quiet weekend in Manila. The mornings were comfortably cool as the warm summer days of March approached. The dry season had already begun. The weather was to play its part in the success of the upheaval.

At Malacañang, the Palace hummed with activity as carpenters set up a stage on the grounds for the inauguration of Marcos on February 25, at high noon as tradition bade. Deputy Minister of Public Works Aber Canlas was supervising construction work outside the Maharlika building. Workers were festooning the Palace with the customary red-white-and-blue decorations. Information Minister Gregorio S. Cendaña appeared too busy to look after "the boys," the reporters covering the President. Normally, he would take them to the President's study room where Marcos would tell them he had "time for two or three questions." But the reporters were busy. They had been sniffing rumors flying around and were now checking one out: that martial law was about to be declared. Apparently, they had missed out on the significance of six tanks and two armored personnel carriers, plus the somewhat unusual number of soldiers in and outside the premises. Did they perhaps think that these signs had to do with security preparations for the inauguration?

★ ★ ★

Actually, the concentration of military forces within and around Malacañang was more than what was needed for the President's security in an inaugural ceremony. Besides these forces, there were others close by, poised to reinforce the Malacañang troops on signal from Ver.

The day before, Ver had pulled out the 14th Infantry Battalion from Nueva Ecija, a province about a hundred kilometers north of Manila, with orders to rush to Malacañang.

At 2 a.m. on Saturday, February 22, Ver ordered the 5th Marine Battalion Landing Team out of Zamboanga, on Mindanao island 700 kilometers south of Manila, to fly to the national capital and join the Malacañang forces.

From Camp Aquino in Tarlac, 110 kilometers north of Manila, Ver plucked 8 officers and 82 enlisted personnel from the 5th Infantry Battalion in Piddig, Ilocos Norte, Marcos' home province on the northwestern tip of Luzon, for urgent posting in Malacañang.

Furthermore, Ver had one Philippine Air Force Crowd Dispersal and Control Battalion to beef up the anti-riot units protecting Malacañang.

The sudden troop movements were evident to military men who could see through the impetuous Ver, who had hardly any combat experience in a life almost entirely dedicated to the protection of Marcos.

★ ★ ★

Normally, the Presidential Security Command (PSC) which is a division size conglomerate of specially trained troops with supporting components from the Air Force, the Navy, the Army, and the Constabulary, would be adequate even in an emergency situation, to protect the President and the seat of government. The PSC commanding general was Brig. Gen. Santiago Barangan. Actual control of the force, however, was in the hands of General Ver's son, Col. Irwin Ver, the

PSC chief of staff. Two other sons of Ver were in that private army of Marcos, but none of the Ver sons, like their father, had any combat experience. But they had been heard to declare that they were willing to stake their lives for Marcos, a relative of their father.

Malacañang's defenses were divided into four sectors. The Palace as well as Gates 1 and 2, were in Sector 1, the responsibility of Col. Irwin Ver. The administration building as well as Gates 3 and 4 were in Sector 2 under the First Security Battalion of the PSC headed by Col. Nestor Santillan. Lt. Col. Arsenio Tecson's 2nd Battalion covered Sector 4 with jurisdiction over the officer's quarters, the Presidential Command headquarters and the Central Park. Sector 3, which included the fenced inner park, the golf course, gymnasium, General Ver's quarters, and the Community Hall, was assigned also to Irwin Ver.

The Pasig River, from its mouth at Manila Bay to Guadalupe about two kilometers from the Palace, was secured by a Philippine Navy unit composed of six patrol craft fast, two frigates, a demolition team, and ferry boats. Like each of the four sectors, the Navy Palace Command had a battalion of ground troops.

Lt. Col. Rexor Ver headed the Presidential Security Unit, composed of 400 men whose primary mission was to provide close-in security to the First Family. The Recon company of the PSC, an armored unit under Major Wyrlo Ver, had 8 light Scorpion tanks, 10 M-113 Armored Personnel Carriers (APC), and 11 V150s.

All approaches to the Palace by road were secured by the Metrocom Western Sector under Lt. Col. Agapito Heredia. This unit was operationally under the Presidential Security Command, a highly mobile unit with 350 men that took care of the choke points at the Ayala-Lozano approach, the Sta. Mesa-J.P. Laurel approach, the Mendiola approach, and all approaches on Otis street and Nagtahan bridge. The unit was also assigned to provide the Palace with in-depth defense.

The First Coast Guard District, almost a battalion in strength, was operationally under the Navy Palace Command. Navy Capt. Carmelo Santos commanded both the Navy Palace Command and the Coast Guard Unit. All in all, they had 3,629 fully armed officers and men.

★   ★   ★

On February 19, three days before Day 1 of the revolution, Colonel Ver placed the Presidential Security Command on red alert. This surprised his subordinates, but he merely hinted at an "impending attack" on the Palace. He did not give any details. Neither did he discuss any plan of defense. As it happened, a Tactical Operations Center (TOC) was set up that very day by General Ver at the Community Hall in anticipation of the attack, but nothing happened.

The tension eased, and everything was quiet among the military units in and around the Palace. Although there was an unusual concentration of military strength there, nobody except the Vers and the brasshats close to them would have thought of the possibility of an attack on the Palace.

It had never crossed their minds that in a few days, a psychological bombshell would be exploded by Enrile and Ramos.

★   ★   ★

There was no sign of worry on the faces of General Ver and Mrs. Imelda Romualdez Marcos, the First Lady, as they stood as sponsors at the wedding of Major Gen. Vicente Piccio's son, Philip, at the Villamor Air Base chapel. Piccio was the Philippine Air Force commanding general. But somewhere during the wedding rites, Ver and the First Lady learned of the Enrile-Ramos break and hurriedly skipped the reception at the Manila Hotel so they could make their way post-haste to Malacañang.

At Malacañang, reporters covering the Palace beat had been wait-ing all afternoon for a chance to see Marcos. Visitors came and went. Among the politicians who saw the President, there was talk that Enrile had filed a request with the Ministry of Foreign Affairs for the revalidation of his and his family's passports. Another rumor had the minister preparing his irrevocable resignation, which he would formal-ly submit to Marcos on Monday, February 24.

★ ★ ★

Although the reporters did not notice the overflow of military strength that poured into the Palace premises and its surroundings, they alerted their news desks to a big story that just might break. They had a feeling that Marcos was about to declare martial law again. A military reporter had already heard about "Oplan Everlasting," a list of the people to be arrested in the event that martial law was declared. On the list were presidential candidate Corazon C. Aquino and oppo-sition party leaders. Also on the list: Enrile and Ramos. Reporters were unable to obtain confirmation from either Marcos or Ver, but they were sure that martial law was in the air when they came upon a foreign wire dispatch quoting Mrs. Cristina Ponce Enrile, the minister's wife, as saying that she had been told that her husband was about to be arrested.

★ ★ ★

An indication that Marcos' mind was not at ease that day was that he gave orders that his entire family should be at the Palace. The military fetched daughter Imee and her husband Tommy Manotoc and their children from their home in Wack Wack, Mandaluyong, and daughter Irene, husband Greggy Araneta, and their children from their home in

Forbes Park, Makati. Later came son Bongbong (Ferdinand Jr.) who soon donned a fatigue uniform, reminiscent of the days when he trained as a jungle fighter. The First Lady attempted a facade of calm, but she was obviously fidgety.

On top of Marcos' anxiety over the threat of civil disobedience poised by the opposition was the constant feeding of information from Ver about the security situation, information which was nevertheless clouded by uncertainties. The President depended on Ver for information on what was going on. The general leaned on Marcos for the decision on what was to be done. What Ver and Marcos were continually talking about that Saturday, nobody among the officers and enlisted personnel in Malacañang knew, except perhaps Col. Irwin Ver. Even the personal bodyguards of Marcos' children did not know what was going on; they learned of the Enrile-Ramos breakaway only from a delayed telecast.

★ ★ ★

For Mrs. Enrile and Mrs. Ramos, who were used to the cares and anxieties of soldiers' wives, that historic Saturday when the revolution began was an ordinary day.

That morning, Enrile left his house at Dasmariñas Village and went to the Atrium in Makati for breakfast with a motley group of politicians, businessmen, and journalists. He said nothing to indicate an impending break with Marcos. He even had a few good words for the President. He was taking part in a lively discussion when Lt. Noelo Albano, his aide, handed him a note. After a while, he excused himself from the group.

Trade and Industry Minister Roberto Ongpin was on the phone with an urgent message that 19 of his security men had been arrested by Marines while on night training exercises at Fort Bonifacio.

"Why?" he asked Ongpin.

"I don't know, but these men had been training at night time for the past year in full battle gear," Ongpin said.

"I'll check and ring you back," Enrile assured Ongpin.

Enrile was worried because three of those men, all military personnel, were from his office and on loan to Ongpin to train his own security force.

A few minutes later, Brig. Gen. Jaime Alfonso, his senior military executive assistant, was on the line. The minister excused himself again from the coffee drinkers to answer the phone. Alfonso's report: "They were conducting VIP security training in the Philippine Marine area with prior coordination with the Marine staff officers and at the time of their apprehension, they were already on their fourth night of training this week." He added that the Military Police Brigade was conducting a formal investigation on the incident.

★ ★ ★

Enrile went back to the table, bade his friends goodbye, and went straight home. He had a quick lunch with Cristina and some guests.

He had barely stood up from his chair when Col. Gregorio Honasan and Lt. Col. Eduardo Kapunan, his chief security and intelligence officer, respectively, rushed in with the news they had been expecting all along: Marcos' ordering the arrest of Enrile, Ramos, Reformist officers, and some opposition leaders.

In Enrile's bedroom, Honasan and Kapunan reviewed with Enrile their plans to meet the contingency. Meantime, Maj. Noe Wong, the minister's senior military aide-de-camp, showed up to say that the contingency plan had leaked. "It's all right," Kapunan said as he looked at some maps. What Kapunan could not tell Wong was that the leak was part of their strategy to deceive the enemy.

The Reformists had two options in their contingency plan. The "benign" option, or Plan A, was to engage the forces of Marcos and Ver in a struggle for legal, peaceful, and constitutional reforms through the use of the chain of command in the armed forces. The "naughty" option, or Plan B, was to go on "war footing" if Plan A could not bring about the reforms sought. The Reformists would then have to take a "symbolic" stand and go down fighting to save the country and establish a military tradition for future generations.

The "naughty" option had many scenarios, each designed to meet a particular situation as the fight developed. There was the possibility of Enrile making a stand in Cagayan, whose people and terrain he is familiar with, not only as a native of the place but also as a young guerrilla during the Japanese occupation. Simultaneously, there would be guerrilla fighting in Manila, to make life unbearable for the leaders of the regime. There would also be resistance activities in Bicol, the Visayas, and Mindanao, the resistance to snowball until it crushes the regime. The Reformists had kept 1,000 barrels of aviation fuel in seven RAM bases in these areas for guerrilla operations while they were training.

Another aspect of Plan B was a commando raid on Malacañang to take possession of the persons of Marcos and his wife in the event Enrile and Ramos were arrested.

In that event, Enrile, Ramos, and the security group of the minister were to make a stand at Camp Aguinaldo and neighboring Camp Crame. If they would be wiped out, the incident would be expected to spark a revolution. But before they would be vanquished, they would hold Marcos and his wife hostage, while the revolution escalated in ferocity.

★ ★ ★

All options reviewed, Enrile and the officers decided to hurry to Camp Aguinaldo. But first, he had to get in touch with Ramos by phone. The conversation took only a minute:

JPE — Eddie, we are in this condition. We are about to be rounded up. Will you join us?

FVR — Do not use this phone, Sir, because this is not a clear phone. But I am with you all the way.

JPE — Then let us meet at Camp Aguinaldo.

It was 2:30 p.m. Enrile bade a hasty adieu to his wife and gave her directions on what to do for the family's safety.

He was already in his car and about to leave for Camp Aguinaldo when he remembered he also had to get in touch with Jaime Cardinal Sin, Archbishop of Manila. The minister rushed back to his room and asked his wife to call the cardinal, and inform him of the impending arrests. Then he left.

★ ★ ★

When Enrile called, Ramos was in the thick of a dialogue with a crowd of Cory's Crusaders who had been picketing his house at Alabang Hills since morning. One placard screamed: "Ramos resign!" Another commanded: "Remember the Escalante massacre." This had reference to a shootout in Escalante, a town in Negros Occidental, where Constabulary soldiers were implicated in the killing of 27 civilians. Ramos was chief of Constabulary at the time, and detractors were making every effort to pin the blame on him. Enrile had ordered the carnage investigated by a bipartisan panel, which then came out with a report that cleared Ramos, although a few members expressed the view during the panel's deliberation that Ramos had to answer for "negligence." It was this minority view that was emphasized in a press release issued by an officer under the control of Ver.

The general requested Mrs. Ramos to carry on with the dialogue, begged leave of the crowd, and sped to Camp Aguinaldo.

★ ★ ★

Cardinal Sin was not in his Palace at the time Mrs. Enrile called up, but the minister's wife was able to talk to him later through Sister Josefina. The cardinal assured Mrs. Enrile he would do something to help the minister. He also told Mrs. Enrile she could use his palace as a sanctuary for the family in case she would need one.

The cardinal received a similar call from Mrs. Betty Go-Belmonte, co-chairman of the *Philippine Daily Inquirer*, who had been contacted by Mrs. Enrile. The cardinal's reaction, which was to set the tone for the uniquely Christian response to the Marcos juggernaut poised against Camp Aguinaldo, was to call for prayers.

He called the contemplative sisters. The Manila archdiocese has three in the metropolis — the Poor Claire Sisters, the Pink Sisters, and the Carmelite Sisters. The cardinal told them: "Come out from your cells. Go immediately to the chapel and before the exposed Blessed Sacraments with outstretched arms, you have to pray and prostrate before God on the floor. And you should start fasting tonight, and you should not eat solid food until the time when I will tell you, because we are in battle and you are the powerhouses. And the moment we do not win the battle, you will have to fast until the end of your life."

Then he appealed to the people to go to Camp Aguinaldo.

★ ★ ★

It was 3 p.m. when Enrile and his party arrived at Camp Aguinaldo, the largest piece of real estate owned by the government in Quezon City. In the center of the camp facing Bonny Serrano is the GHQ building where the armed forces chief of staff holds office. At a corner to the left is the Ministry of National Defense (MND) building. Beside the MND building and almost to the immediate left of GHQ is the home of the Intelligence Service of the Armed Forces of the Philippines, or ISAFP. Behind these are other installations such as the Logistics Command which is adjacent to a poor residential area known as Libis. Behind the GHQ are many other installations among which is the KKK (livelihood project) building which symbolizes the military commitment to the Marcos-Imelda program of promoting backyard farming and home industries. There is also an area called the Enlisted Men's Village where soldiers live with their families. A large area of the camp is dedicated to a golf course, among the better ones in the city. Across EDSA from Camp Aguinaldo is Camp Crame, home of the Philippine Constabulary and only about a third of the size of Camp Aguinaldo. It has a four-story headquarters building, a station hospital, an athletic field and parade grounds, a gymnasium, a chapel, and a housing area.

★ ★ ★

Enrile upon arrival instructed his information officer to call a press conference — it was to be a "big one" because foreign correspondents were in town to cover the inauguration of Marcos as well as the inauguration of Mrs. Aquino (the opposition held on to their belief that their presidential bet had won the elections). The press conference was set to start at 6:30 p.m. Newsmen were told by the MND press office: "Expect something big."

★ ★ ★

There was much to do before the journalists would start streaming in. Enrile's security group made haste to get organized and deploy to protect the MND building and its occupants.

Two helicopters — a Sikorsky and a Bolkow — landed on the front lawn of the ministry building. They had just sneaked out of Villamor Air Base with a load of armaments for the "Cagayan 100" contingent that had been spirited out of Enrile's home province to beef up Enrile's defenses at Camp Aguinaldo.

These choppers constituted part of a small unit called the Office of the Minister of National Defense Aviation Group under the command of Col. Ciriaco S. Reconquista. Now, part of this unit was in Camp Aguinaldo while another was in Villamor Air Base (VAB) which was "enemy territory" to the rebels. The VAB portion which included Reconquista did intelligence gathering at the base for Camp Crame and underground arrangements for reception of defectors at the camp.

Evidently suspected by top PAF brass to be a rebel, Reconquista was prohibited from taking off in any aircraft. Piccio himself advised him: "Ike, do not make any move in your area because everytime you make a move there, you make people here (at headquarters) tense."

Led by the Cagayan Constabulary provincial commander, Col. Tirso Gador, the "Cagayan 100" was to play an important role in the revolution. Now fully armed, the Cagayan contingent took up positions to secure the ministry building."

The first military region to go to the rebel side was Regional Unified Command No. 8 which included troops in Mrs. Marcos own province, Leyte. It was a fortunate coincidence for Enrile that on the first day of the revolution, RUC-8 commander, Brig. Gen. Salvador Mison, was with his family in Camp Aguinaldo. When Enrile began calling RUC chiefs to ask them which side they were on, he had Mison first in mind because he was within the camp.

Mison rushed from his quarters and reported to the minister. Enrile put the question to him and his immediate reply was: "Sir, I have always been with you, and there is absolutely no reason why I should back out now. I am at your orders."

"All right, get hold of your men and alert them for any eventuality," the defense chief said.

At 5:45 p.m., Mison went back to his quarters, got his chief of staff, Col. Joselin Nazareno, in Tacloban City on the phone, and gave him instructions.

★ ★ ★

After inquiring on the preparation for the press conference, Enrile placed an overseas telephone call to former Executive Secretary Rafael Salas in New York, where Salas holds office as deputy secretary general of the United Nations. He briefly apprised Salas of the situation and the developments thus far, and then asked Salas to take care of his (Enrile's) family should anything happen to him. Then he requested Salas to "please inform our friends in the United Nations that we are in this kind of situation."

★　★　★

He remembered the request of Minister Roberto Ongpin. He asked his security chief, Colonel Honasan, to fetch Brig. Gen. Pedro Balbanero, the Military Police Brigade commander, from his office at Camp Aguinaldo.

Balbanero had under his custody the 19 persons, led by Lt. (sg) Michael Aspirin, a Reformist, the subject of Ongpin's request. They were arrested Saturday morning by elements of the Philippine Marines in an off-limits area at Fort Bonifacio doing night road run training in combat attire, fully armed. Only three in the group were military personnel; the rest were civilians. The Marines thought they were spying on the restricted area.

The capture of the group worried Enrile because among the captives were his own security men whom he had detailed with Ongpin. A report on the incident could have reached General Ver, and the latter could very well misinterpret it, considering it concerned Enrile. It could lead to a premature discovery of the goings-on at Camp Aguinaldo.

★　★　★

Honasan fetched General Balbanero. But on their way to the minnistry building, Balbanero was astonished to see fully armed soldiers in the premises of the building. He asked Honasan, "Greg, where are your people bound for?"

"Oh, just an operation, Sir." Honasan replied, trying hard to sound casual.

At the ministry Social Hall where Enrile was waiting for the newspapermen to come for the press conference, Balbanero saw retired Generals Romeo C. Espino, former AFP chief of staff, and Manuel T. Flores, former superintendent of the Philippine Military Academy.

Without hesitation, Enrile laid his cards on the table and briefed Balbanero. It was, for both men, a make-or-break situation. Balbanero could turn Enrile in and arrest his men, or he could support them in this critical hour.

Balbanero was "shocked and speechless" for a while. Then he told the minister he knew of no order to arrest the Reformists. Besides, if the minister had any doubts that the capture of Aspirin's group was indicative of a plan to arrest Enrile, Ramos, and the Reformists, the matter had just been settled. Balbanero gave the minister a copy of his report on the Aspirin incident, but sensed that "apparently, (Enrile) was not convinced."

Just then, Balbanero saw Col. Rolando Abadilla, Metrocom intelligence chief, and the idea came to him that he and Abadilla could arrange for Enrile to see Marcos and General Ver in Malacañang for a dialogue. Enrile talked to Abadilla and permitted Balbanero and Abadilla to go to Malacañang.

★ ★ ★

Meanwhile, the presence of fully armed men around, inside, and atop the ministry building attracted the intelligence personnel at the neighboring ISAFP building. But there were Reformists in ISAFP and

Enrile's security group was not worried about any hostile action from that direction.

But Col. Rodolfo Estrellado of ISAFP was curious about the goings-on at the ministry building. He went over, learned of the scheduled press conference, and reported it to his chief, Brig. Gen. Fidel Singson, who then instructed him to keep quiet until he (Singson) could come to check it out.

★ ★ ★

Balbanero and Abadilla arrived at Malacañang at about 5 p.m. that Saturday. Ver was still with the First Lady at the Villamor Air Base chapel where they stood as sponsors at the Piccio wedding. Half an hour later, Ver arrived. He was shocked and could not believe what Balbanero and Abadilla had to tell him. He left them for a few minutes and came back to inform Balbanero and Abadilla that Marcos wanted to talk with Enrile.

From Malacañang, Balbanero tried to reach Enrile by phone. After 30 minutes, he gave up. Balbanero and Abadilla then rushed back to Camp Aguinaldo.

★ ★ ★

There was already a big crowd around Enrile and Ramos waiting for the press conference to begin. Balbanero gave Enrile Marcos' message. Enrile replied, "Pete, we have already burned our bridges."

Abadilla tried to convince Enrile to call Marcos.

Enrile said, "I'm sorry, I think we have reached a point where capitulation is out of the question and we will not surrender."

Abadilla went on to say that from what he had gathered from Malacañang, Marcos did not really intend to harm him or Ramos. The intention was only to arrest Enrile's security men implicated in a plot on Marcos' life.

Enrile firmly brushed aside the idea: "No, I cannot call the President."

★ ★ ★

Abadilla left. After a while, he returned. It was the same message. Marcos wanted to see Enrile.

The reply was still "no."

Abadilla offered, "Would you then speak with General Ver, Sir?"

This is part of the Enrile-Ver conversation:

JPE — What is it, Fabian?

Ver — Minister, we never had any intention to harm your group and we cannot understand why you reacted that way, etc.

JPE — Well, anyway we are in this condition. Why don't we talk in the morning about this and maybe we can find a solution to this unpleasant problem. Just don't allow your men to approach our area so that there will be no incident.

Ver — You must also tell your men not to attack the Palace.

JPE — No, we will not attack the Palace. You have my word. We have no intention of attacking the Palace.

Thus, at sundown on Saturday, February 22, even before Enrile and Ramos announced their point-of-no-return, Malacañang knew about it, to the extent that Ver established with the Enrile-Ramos camp a modus vivendi by which contact and hostile action between the two groups would be avoided.

★ ★ ★

After his talk with Ver, Enrile was happy. If there was anything his camp needed most at that point, it was time. And it was time his conversation with Ver bought. But he was also apprehensive. A truce is a gentleman's agreement; it will hold only if both parties to the agreement remained gentlemen.

He told his men not to relax their guard.

Ver probably was the more insecure of the two, and it was from him that trouble could come, Enrile told himself.

Enrile could figure out Ver's bewilderment, which forced him to sue for temporary peace with the Enrile-Ramos camp, telling Enrile, "You must tell your men not to attack the Palace."

Six days before the breakaway, on a Sunday, the Reformists leaked details of a supposed plot to kidnap the President and the First Lady and force them on their knees to step down from the presidency. It was a hoax, designed to test the reaction of Marcos bodyguards. It was just one of the naughty "electrocutions" the Reformists were dishing out to Ver's intelligence agents.

What Enrile feared was that Ver might undertake a preemptive move by ignoring the truce and ordering a strike at Camp Aguinaldo.

★   ★   ★

Meanwhile, Balbanero decided to play a "neutral" role so he could continue to be an emissary between the two camps. But his troops, which by that time were the only ones inside Camp Aguinaldo that could take hostile action against the Enrile-Ramos group, were advised by the Reformists to keep their distance.

★   ★   ★

It was 6:30 p.m. The press conference started. Enrile wore a long-sleeved fatigue jacket over a bullet-proof vest, denim pants, and rubber sneakers. Ramos was in a gray short-sleeved jacket without any military insignia, pants to match, and leather shoes. He laid aside his favorite pipe for a cigar. Both men wore a facade of calm, but to the newsmen's chorus of "Good evening," Enrile said, "Thank you. I do not know whether this will be a good evening. But anyway, we are ready to answer your questions."

The principal points he and Ramos wanted to put across:

I

Regarding the impending arrests, information was that he, Ramos, and members of the Reform Movement would be arrested by the Presidential Security Command on orders of the "highest authority" (President Marcos). That was why they were gathered at Camp Aguinaldo, to take a defensive position and preempt the impending arrests. "If there is going to be any shooting, it is not going to start from us here. If we have to die, we die here," Enrile said.

II

Regarding their withdrawal of support for the Marcos regime, "I have been searching my mind, my heart, and my conscience and my soul for many days even before the proclamation of Marcos, whether it is worth my time to support a government that, in my opinion, with full knowledge of the election frauds, did not represent the will of the Filipino people. Personally, I think Marcos did not really win this election. . . I have been associated with him for over 21 years, and I was affected by a moral dilemma, my loyalty to a man whom I considered a friend, and my loyalty to my country. And I said to myself, I must serve my country first, ahead of anyone else."

Ramos concurred: "I wish to make it clear on my part, and the minister certainly has said it on his part, that we are withdrawing our support for Mr. Marcos and all his cohorts. We do not recognize his proclaimed presidency and the rest of his government as representing the people. They are not to me the duly constituted authorities of this country under the Constitution."

III

Regarding the deterioration of the armed forces, Enrile said: "I cannot in conscience recognize Marcos as Commander-in-Chief of the armed forces . . . The Armed Forces of the Philippines is no longer the armed forces of the people as it should be. There is already an attitude on the part of some people that they own the armed forces, they own the country, they own everybody. They say that Ver was retired on a Sunday only to be reinstated again, then only to be retired again after which General Ramos was announced to be the acting chief of staff. But there is a secret order saying that Ver must continue as chief of staff until such time as his retirement would be announced. We can no longer live under this condition. This is no longer a civilized country if this is the way they are running our affairs.

"I am no longer privy to their planning. They are putting people in the military command without consultation with us or with General Ramos. And I felt that this is no longer a Ministry of National Defense. It's simply a decoration. We are deodorants, without anything to do . . . It is written in the law that the ministry selects and recommends to the President the officers who will be raised to the rank of brigadier general but the law was totally disregarded.

"The division within the military began a long time ago because of discrimination in promotions, assignments, appointments, schooling privileges. I think it is inevitable that this will lead to this showdown.

"The most unfortunate thing that happened in this country is that the President listened only to people who were able to reach him and these people have their own vested interests to protect. In our case, we tried to make the military organization a professional organization beholden not to a man but to the Filipino people so that they can protect the common weal and the interests of our country. But we could not do anything about it."

Ramos: "I came here because of my sincere conviction that the time has come to reverse the dismal situation. It had been building up in my perception that General Ver and the President are bent on perpetuating themselves in power, by their flip-flopping statements and by their pre-positioning of officers of the armed forces without consultation with the minister of national defense and myself in my capacity as chief of a major service and vice chief of staff, later designated by the President as acting chief of staff with clipped authority. But on top of that, I came here to support the decision of Minister Enrile to seek a better armed forces for which I feel partly responsible, and a better overall life for our people.

"Mr. Marcos has been President for 20 years and I was with the armed forces even before he assumed that high office. I have gone through all the levels of command from platoon leader to chief of major service, including stints in the campaign against the communist *Hukbalahap*, in Korea, in Vietnam, and in the 1972 martial law situation. Now, there are many officers close to General Ver who did not do anything except to be assigned in Malacañang and to travel back and forth from the Palace and abroad during the period of hardship of our armed forces in the '70s. Yet they have risen to very high ranks not because of what they know or what they have done, but because of their closeness to the President and to General Ver. Some of them hold multiple positions as if they are the only ones who are good in the armed forces. During my stint as acting chief of staff for 13 months, I tried to eliminate these pernicious practices. But I can only go so far because of the limited authority granted me by the President."

Ramos said he saw the building of an elite military group — including a spy net — by Ver as incompatible with professionalism and as an instrument for the perpetuation of Marcos and Ver in power.

Ramos told the press conference: "The people in this elite group are in positions not only of command but also of procurement and in finance within the armed forces. They are also very much in intelligence. I think we should watch out for the connection between the National Intelligence and Security Authority (NISA) and this elite group. Armed forces authorities are kept in the dark about NISA activities. Many of our personnel are utilized by the NISA without the knowledge of proper authority. And the activities and operations of NISA have already infringed upon law enforcement and even other activities that properly belong to other agencies of the government and, therefore, they have gone beyond the authority granted by law to an intelligence and security authority. The elite group and the NISA have become a virtual Gestapo spying on every corner of the government down to the lowest local unit.

"Let me tell you about Brig. Gen. Tomas Dumpit, the regional unified commander of Region I who also commands the PC-INP (Philippine Constabulary-Integrated National Police) in the same region. I charged him, I wrote the President almost three years ago and accused General Dumpit of being involved in massive carnaping in which several of his officers at this time were involved. They all belong to the PSC. We documented these charges. We have witnesses to support the case. But in the long run, after the material was submitted to the President, the entire thing was whitewashed and our witnesses began to disappear one by one. This is just one instance where a member of the elite group got away with crime."

Ramos complained that Marcos used his name as an assurance that the elections would be clean when Constabulary and Police officers were being pushed around by politicians close to Marcos: "I became very, very disappointed with the President when he continued to use my name as a cosmetic, a deodorant to help prop up his regime. He announced to the world that as chief of Constabulary and director general of the Integrated National Police, I would be responsible for the clean and orderly conduct of the election. What bites me is the fact that while he gave me this responsibility, some of his political leaders, with his consent, pressured some military people in their localities to issue firearms to their followers to facilitate the perpetration of acts of political terrorism and fraud. This has made me realize that he gave me a hot potato without any authority with which to handle it. On top of that, he was actively undermining my efforts to ensure an honest, orderly, and peaceful election."

Ramos named some of those politicians: Roberto Benedicto, Eduardo Cojuangco, Benjamin Romualdez, Ali Dimaporo, and Armando Gustilo, "all of whom received a lot of firearms without the knowledge of those who are in the chain of command."

Ramos said that although he was breaking off from the Marcos regime, "I am making myself available to serve the armed forces of the people and the Integrated National Police of the people."

IV

Regarding the significance of the impending arrests, Enrile said that as far as he and Ramos were concerned, they saw no legal basis for these. Nevertheless, from his experience with the declaration of martial law in 1972, mass arrests were a necessary instrument of the regime.

Enrile said, "I would like to address this to the President, that if in his opinion we have violated the laws, he should bring us to trial and I am willing to meet him in court. I am a lawyer by profession . . . I am going to show at the trial what happened to this country in the past 20 years under his regime so the people will know the whole truth. I will do it as a service to the Filipino people if it is the last thing that I must do."

The minister recalled that there was a meeting in the Palace about 3 or 4 days before. Generals were summoned to Malacañang where Marcos instructed them to prepare contingency plans to be implemented in case of public disorder. Marcos evidently feared that the civil disobedience movement of Mrs. Aquino and the opposition could develop into real trouble for the regime.

Enrile said he was not invited to the meeting but Ramos was. Ver and the other crony generals were there, too. Ramos said there was a plan to arrest Mrs. Aquino and all her 50 advisers. Also in the arrest list were members of the Reform Movement. Enrile and Ramos were not in the list but then they were with the Movement. Mrs. Aquino was not listed, either, but Ramos said Minister Ongpin had informed him that she would be arrested. Apparently, there was another list that named Enrile, Ramos, and Mrs. Aquino.

Asked if he would resist another declaration of martial law, Enrile replied emphatically, "I will, because it is going to be against the interests of our people . . . The people will not accept it and he (Marcos) will face an open civil war in this land. I doubt whether he can impose martial law at this time. If the President will miscalculate the situation, there will follow an outbreak of violence."

The Harvard-educated lawyer said he regretted his participation in the 1972 declaration of martial law. "Had I known that martial law would be installed to repress our people, I would not have agreed to its imposition. When we discussed the imposition of martial law, it was for a noble purpose, which was to stabilize the situation in our land. But later on, it was corrupted and used for a purpose other than what we had intended it in the beginning."

He pointed to General Espino who was then chief of staff and who was present at the press conference to bear witness. If Mrs. Enrile were present, at that time, she would also have confirmed her husband's disillusionment with martial law which he thought would last for a few years only. Midway in that ten-year period of repression, Enrile perceived that martial law was being utilized for the aggrandizement of Marcos and his cronies and of Ver and his elite corps.

On the impending arrests, Ramos commented, "Well, I am calling on all members of the Armed Forces of the Philippines and the Integrated National Police to disobey all illegal orders of whoever is giving them. I consider any assault on the people, the firing upon unarmed and unprotected civilians as partaking of illegal orders. Also the unjustified arrest of leaders just because they espouse opposite political beliefs from those of President Marcos, to me constitute illegal order. Illegal too is the entire spectrum of unjust and unfair actions which the Marcos regime is prone to do."

V

Regarding the possibility of negotiations with Marcos and Ver, Enrile said, "I am willing to talk to Mr. Marcos and explain our position. But I don't think I should go to the Palace. That would be like going inside a prison camp."

Ramos was also in a negotiating mood. "I am willing to dialogue with the President to express the feelings of those in the Armed Forces of the Philippines. In fact, that is my primary and only approach. I am making myself available for negotiations, consultations, and advice with those who are willing to talk to me. And that includes the President."

★ ★ ★

Enrile and Ramos welcomed negotiations because they needed time for all officers and enlisted personnel in the armed forces to finally find their conscience and switch support to their side. Time was also needed for the people to rally to their support.

Enrile and Ramos calculated that Marcos was as eager as they were to have the matter peacefully settled but the road could only lead to a dead-end because one important point was non-negotiable. They would not mention this to Marcos until the appropriate moment. This was for Marcos to step down from the presidency.

VI

Regarding Mrs. Aquino, Enrile made it clear that she had nothing to do with their decision. She was at the time in Cebu to drum up support for her civil disobedience movement. Here are portions of the conference transcript:

Question — Did you have any contact with Mrs. Aquino?

JPE — We have not had any contact with Mrs. Aquino.

Q — Mr. Minister, are you willing to accept the authority of Mrs. Aquino as President?

JPE — I am not making any conclusion. Whoever is considered by the Filipino people to be the representative of their will must be respected.

Q — Are you willing to talk with Mrs. Aquino about this situation?

JPE — Well, I suppose at this point that anybody who would support us is welcome.

Q — Are you going to stay and serve under Mrs. Aquino if she is installed as President?

JPE — I am talking of a country and people and not of men to whom we owe loyalty. Our loyalty is to the Constitution, to the Filipino people, to our country . . . I am not interested in power, or position, in the government. I am not doing this because I want glory or wealth or power. I am doing this as a matter of duty and obligation to our people.

Q — Mr. Enrile, if you believe Mrs. Aquino was duly elected, will you support her?

JPE — I am morally convinced that it was Mrs. Aquino who was elected by the Filipino people. Yes, we are committed to support her.

Q — Will you be willing to join a government under Mrs. Aquino?

JPE — I have not made up my mind.

VII

Since Enrile and Ramos had no intention at all to seize power it would be a misnomer to call the action a coup d'etat.

VIII

Regarding support from a foreign government, Enrile was emphatic that the decision that he and Ramos took was purely and independently their own. But they wanted the world to sympathize with them in their plight. The minister said, "I am calling on the people of the world to help us restore decency, justice, freedom, and real democracy in this land, because there is no justice, there is no decency, and there is no real freedom, much less democracy in this hapless land."

He added, "We appeal to the people of the world to help us in this situation. We can no longer appeal to reason among our leaders. I think world opinion must be brought to bear to resolve the problems of our land, and if we should succumb to this fateful undertaking, then let history judge us. Historians on this nation will be kinder to us than to those who will annihilate us."

Enrile said nobody had as yet indicated any help. "We are going to help ourselves, even with our bare hands . . . For me, it is more honorable now to be killed by this regime than to fight and die for it."

IX

Although he called up the ambassadors of the United States and of Japan soon after his coming to his office, Enrile said this was merely to inform them of the situation he and Ramos were in.

Enrile added: "I am almost tempted to anticipate that the President will probably mobilize now his propaganda machine to paint us as tools of foreign interests. We are not. We are not acting at the behest or under the influence of anyone. We are acting in accordance with our conscience as Filipinos. We are involved in protecting and serving the interests of our people."

X

On support from the people, Enrile replied, "It's up to them if they want to support us. We are here to make a stand."

On mass action in the streets as an expression of support. "Even if we are not supported by the people, we have taken a stand, and so be it. After all, life is God's gift. It is only He who will take it. Even with all the guns arrayed against us, if God's will is to spare us, He will spare us."

Asked whether he had any message for the people, Enrile had this to say: "I am asking the Filipino people to wake up to what is happening in our land and I am asking the members of the armed forces who believe in the oath that they have taken to preserve and defend the Constitution, to do just that. We are not asking for any harm to anybody, but that we must obey the laws and not the will of the man whose mandate is in serious doubt."

Ramos said their appeal would be heard throughout the land because Radio Veritas, the Voice of America, and other radio stations in the city were broadcasting it. Already there were appeals aired on radio to the people to bring food and water to Camp Aguinaldo and later, Camp Crame.

Enrile, however, was hesitant about calling on the people to come and mass around the camps. (The appeal was made by broadcasters and by members of the religious orders.)

As excerpted from transcript:

Q — Are you calling the people to come or . . .?

JPE — I am asking them to help us.

Q — But how?

JPE — I do not know. It is up to them to decide what has to be done.

Q — You ask whatever you want to ask the people.

JPE — There are many political options available to them. I asked people to contact the other leaders of both political parties and I have also asked that the leaders of the Catholic Church and the National Council of Churches be told about what is happening.

★   ★   ★

Enrile was reluctant to disclose the role of the people in the streets in the crisis because he did not want to divulge to Malacañang any portion of the defense plans for the two camps which Ramos was at the moment figuring out.

A premature disclosure would have been dangerous, because "people power" was going to be an element in the defense strategy.

★ ★ ★

For the fastest mobilization of popular support, the Enrile-Ramos camp depended heavily on the broadcast media and on the newspapers. Military units throughout the country obtained their information about what was going on at Camp Aguinaldo from radio and TV. Initially the direct link of Enrile and Ramos with the people was Radio Veritas. Later, they established a clandestine radio station in the Santa Mesa area just a couple of kilometers from Malacañang. Worldwide dissemination of information was done by foreign correspondents from the United States, Europe, and Asia.

★ ★ ★

The press conference was over by 8:00 p.m. Ramos left for Camp Crame to establish a defensive position there.

Exactly 45 minutes after the press conference, Brig. Gen. Ramon Farolan, the commissioner of the Bureau of Customs, showed up at Enrile's office and told the remaining newsmen that he was resigning and defecting. Then came Postmaster General Roilo Golez, a Navy man, and elder brother of Ver's aide, who said he was bothered by election fraud and the walkout of the Commission on Elections computer tabulators led by Linda, Colonel Kapunan's wife. He, too, defected. Retired Brig. Gen. Manuel Salientes also showed up and told the minister: "I am here ready to die with you."

Dr. Emmanuel Almeda, Enrile's personal physician, and Member of Parliament Renato Cayetano also arrived. "I am at your service until the end," Almeda told the minister. Then he teamed up with the military doctor of the defense ministry, Lt. Col. Primitivo Rondena. After embracing Cayetano, the minister instructed him to get in touch with some members of the Cabinet and their friends in the Parliament. "Tell them we are in this situation and ask them if they could help us."

In a few minutes, the shockwaves of the Enrile-Ramos initial salvo that shook Malacañang were felt across the nation and around the world.

★ ★ ★

Malacañang reaction was slow. In contrast, defections to the Enrile-Ramos camp were swift, if not entirely silent. They began as soon as the minister arrived at Camp Aguinaldo. Lt. Col. Jerry Albano, commanding officer of the Security Escort Battalion of the Headquarters Service Group, reported that the entire contingent of 200 officers and men were moving over to Enrile's side. Defections of units outside Manila continued throughout the evening and the trend appeared irreversible. The handwriting was on the wall for Malacañang: the danger was real that in the next few days Marcos would be left with no armed forces to be Commander-in-Chief of.

★ ★ ★

From the time Ver ran to him from the wedding at Villamor, Marcos was closeted in his study. At 7 p.m., Malacañang reporters were told that the President was resting. But he was probably awake because Ver and his son Irwin and Information Minister Gregorio Cendaña came and went.

At 7:15 p.m., Ver summoned to his TOC at Malacañang his senior officers, among them, Rear Admiral Brillante Ochoco, the

Navy chief; Brig. Gen. Felix Brawner, deputy chief of staff for opera-
tions and commanding general of the First Scout Ranger Regiment;
Brig. Gen. Jose Bello, deputy for plans and materiels development;
Brig. Gen. Catalino Villanueva, deputy for personnel; Commodore
Serapio Martillano, deputy chief of staff; Brig. Gen. Fortunato Cor-
rachea, deputy for home defense; Navy Capt. Eriberto Varona,
secretary of the general staff; and Col. Irwin Ver, chief of staff of the
PSC.

They talked about military moves against the Enrile-Ramos
group. An officer who saw the TOC said there was not even a situation map in the place. The PSC at the time had 3,629 officers and men
but since their job was to defend Malacañang, Ver had to utilize other
units for the planned operations against the Aguinaldo-Crame complex. There were many units available, including those he had pulled
out of the provinces. At any rate, Ver could not launch an operation in
view of his gentleman's agreement with Enrile that there should be no
contact between their respective forces at least during the night. Balbanero had notified unit commanders of both sides by wire about the
modus vivendi. Ver for his part also notified all military units nationwide that he was still chief of staff of the armed forces. This apparently
was a counter-measure against Ramos' broadcast appeal for them to
ignore Ver.

★ ★ ★

V er placed the entire armed forces on red alert as of midnight. Barbed wire barricades went up along all points of entry to Malacañang.
Ver scheduled another meeting of the generals at the TOC at 3 a.m.
the next day.

At the Malacañang newsroom, reporters were alerted at 8 p.m.
that a televised press conference was set at 10:30 p.m. at the Reception
Hall and they were to be there at 10. They noticed that Deputy
Minister Canlas was still at the grounds outside the old Maharlika
building supervising the construction of the stage for the Marcos inaugural, apparently oblivious of what was happening at Camp Aguinaldo and inside Malacañang. Lights flooded the Palace grounds while

carpenters kept their feverish pace. Inside the Palace, a sign that the situation was not normal was the battle attire of members of the First Family's close-in security unit. Instead of barong Pilipino, they were wearing gray bush jackets.

★ ★ ★

At 8:15 p.m., Brig. Gen. Fidel Singson, chief of ISAFP, received the order from Ver: "Destroy Radio Veritas!"

Ver chose ISAFP to do the job because it was the unit closest to the target station. ISAFP was a next door neighbor of the Ministry of National Defense at Camp Aguinaldo and by that time was preparing to join the Enrile-Ramos forces.

Singson dispatched a team to Veritas with instructions not to take any offensive action but just to reconnoiter the premises. The team reported from the target area that the station was guarded only by two security guards. The team could have easily occupied the station but Singson aborted the mission.

A few minutes later, the ISAFP joined the Enrile-Ramos camp. Thus, there was not one unit in Camp Aguinaldo hostile to Enrile and Ramos. The troops of Balbanero were neutral and about 70 of them were thinking of joining the Reformists.

Ver was infuriated by the inaction of ISAFP on Radio Veritas. He decided to give the task to another force.

★ ★ ★

Meanwhile in Malacañang, the reporters and foreign correspondents were waiting for Marcos' press conference. They saw Mrs. Marcos emerge from the President's study with several politicians, among them former senator Rodolfo Ganzon. She was talking excitedly, in a voice loud enough for the journalists to hear, about the discovery of a "plot" to assassinate her and Marcos at 12:30 a.m.

"We were very lucky," she exclaimed. "There could have been bloodshed. *Nag-panic lang sila* (but they panicked)."

One of the officers in the plot, she said, was Capt. Ricardo Morales, her own chief escort security officer. She mentioned something about the ingratitude of Morales who was a presidential scholar studying at the Asian Institute of Management for a master's degree in business administration.

At 10:00 p.m., Mrs. Marcos was at the Ceremonial Hall to supervise the preparations for the press conference. A small table with pen and paper on it was being carried into the hall and a reporter asked Mrs. Marcos whether that meant Marcos was going to sign something important. She merely smiled and then hastened to remark, "It is there (pointing to the study) where you declare martial law." In a little while the table was brought into the room. This sent reporters to the phone to alert their desks about the possible declaration of martial law.

Mrs. Marcos glided out of the hall whistling a tune.

The press conference, it was decided, would take place in the President's study because the turnout of journalists was not as big as expected. The conference finally began at 10:30 p.m. The Marcos daughters and sons-in-law were present. Imee Marcos-Manotoc and cousin Babes Romualdez supervised the TV crew. Colonel Balbino Diego, legal officer of the Presidential Security Unit, brought in Captain Morales. Off mike, Marcos cautioned reporters not to ask Morales any question. The captain was still under interrogation by his captors.

★ ★ ★

Marcos wore a calm countenance but he looked tired.

He announced that a plot to assassinate him and the First Lady had been uncovered by Colonel Irwin Ver and Governor Ferdinand (Bongbong) Marcos II, the President's son.

Marcos said the assassination was supposed to take place that night (12:30 a.m. as Mrs. Marcos earlier revealed). He called this a coup attempt which was aborted, with the arrest of some officers involved. Quick action on the part of the Presidential Security Unit neutralized three-fourths of the rebel force, according to the President.

Marcos charged Enrile and Ramos with having taken part in the plot. That, he assumed, was the reason they were making their stand at Camp Aguinaldo.

"Their action of supposedly withdrawing their support was a preemptive move to cover up their participation in the plot. I did not know how they could reach this height of treason and rebellion."

That made him "sad," he continued, "and to think that one of them is my relative." (Ramos is a cousin.)

The President presented on television Captain Morales, who he said had a statement to make. Morales fished out a prepared statement from his shirt pocket and read it.

Morales first identified his supposed fellow conspirators Col. Gregorio Honasan, head of Enrile's security group; Major Noe Wong, the minister's aide; Major Arsenio Santos, another aide; Lt. Col. Eduardo Kapunan, Enrile's intelligence chief; Lt. Col. Jake Malajacan, CO of 16 IB of the 2nd Infantry Division; and Major Saulito Aromin, CO of 49 IB, 2nd Infantry Division.

Morales said the plan was to penetrate Malacañang and capture Marcos and his wife. The action was to begin at 12:30 a.m. The attack would be staged from four points. Five commando teams would break through the Palace perimeter from the Pasig River. Malajacan would lead two companies of the 16 IB and an armor company and take diversionary action at Malacañang Park. A Ranger force from the 49 IB would enter Malacañang's gate at J. P. Laurel street in a convoy of six-by-six trucks and a platoon of armor on a ruse that they were reinforcements from Fort Bonifacio. This would be led by Aromin, with his unit from Quezon. The strategem would be credible since Rangers were thought to be loyal to Ver. Kapunan would lead another force and smash through a point behind the Palace gymnasium to cover the commandos clambering up from the river. About three battalions were committed to the operation. All the officers were Reformists.

With an exultant air, Marcos told the press conference the security force in Malacañang would have made mincemeat of the attackers. But they were "neutralized" before they got off the ground because some of the officers were captured and confessed to the plot. However, only Morales, Aromin, Malajacan, and Major Ricardo Brillantes had been arrested. Honasan was leading the defenders at the Aguinaldo sanctuary. Col. Tirso Gador, the Constabulary commander in Enrile's Cagayan province, was named as one of the conspirators. Gador, at the time of Marcos' press conference, was at Camp Aguinaldo leading the "Cagayan 100," a fighting unit pledged to protect Enrile with their lives.

★   ★   ★

Marcos' bluster over the discovery of the coup plot put a smile on the faces of the Reformists at Camp Aguinaldo. There was no such plot to seize power. There was a plan, part of a larger scenario, but it was contingent on the arrest of Enrile and Ramos. If they were arrested and detained at Malacañang, a rescue team would liberate them. And should it become necessary to capture Marcos and his wife in order to extricate Enrile and Ramos, they would do just that. But there was no plan to harm, much less kill, the First Couple.

★   ★   ★

After presenting Morales, Marcos counterattacked on TV. He demanded: "I call upon the *former* minister of national defense and the *former* vice chief of staff to stop this stupidity and surrender so that we may negotiate and decide what will be done with them and their men." (Although he had not fired them publicly, Marcos deliberately referred to Enrile and Ramos as the *former* minister of national defense and the *former* vice chief of staff apparently to impress upon the troops that they were no longer in the service and therefore, should not be obeyed.)

He explained that the claim of Enrile and Ramos that they were about to be arrested was false. There was no warrant of arrest for either of them.

"Now, I know why they took that action. It is because they are among the plotters in a coup which would have been carried out with an assault on Malacañang by Reformist forces led by Col. Gregorio Honasan and the assassination of the President and the First Lady," he said.

Marcos pressed his counterattack. The coup, he said, had been foiled and the forces around Enrile and Ramos were too puny to resist an assult of overwhelming forces that can now be launched against them.

However, as his dialogue with the press wore on, the President became more conciliatory.

"I do not want any bloodshed. I would prefer that you, in that corner of Camp Aguinaldo, surrender. Let us then negotiate," the President addressed Enrile and Ramos directly over television.

At one point, he admitted he found it hard to believe that Minister Enrile and General Ramos were in on the plot.

"Up to now, you will have to convince me." he said.

Marcos insisted before the newsmen that "the situation is under control." He said: "I want to tell you that the armed forces is united behind the President, except for the conspirators supported by parts of isolated companies."

He assured that troops had been organized and poised to liquidate and eliminate the Enrile-Ramos forces and warned that if they were unleashed, "there will be a bloody mess."

Marcos said his loyal forces could wipe out the Enrile-Ramos corner of Camp Aguinaldo with artillery, without any presidential security personnel being involved in the fighting.

"But I would prefer that we talk about how they shall be treated if they surrender," he said.

"Let us handle this with finesse. I have been a soldier myself. I am not the type whose instinct is to kill. My type is to find out why," Marcos was again conciliatory.

But when he was informed by Ver that Ramos had moved to Camp Crame to consolidate forces there, Marcos became agitated anew. He warned over television: "I may not be able to stay from forceful action very long. Ramos should know he is vulnerable to tank and artillery."

The press conference dragged on to about 11:15 p.m. when Imee Marcos-Manotoc advised her father to rest. She accompanied him to another room where she congratulated him for his TV performance.

Morales was escorted out of the conference. As he left, he went over to the First Lady and said, "Madam, we have no intention of killing you and the President."

Mrs. Marcos cried, tapped Morales' right shoulder, and left.

★   ★   ★

By midnight, about fifty thousand people were already milling in all streets surrounding Camp Aguinaldo and Camp Crame, in response to appeals aired over Radio Veritas by the leaders, including Cardinal Sin, Agapito (Butz) Aquino, brother-in-law of Mrs. Aquino, and other concerned citizens.

This was "people power" and its objective was to protect Camp Aguinaldo and Camp Crame with a human barricade that would stop military forces on their way to attack the camps. More and more people from all walks of life, among them priests and nuns, swelled that mass of humanity as the night deepened.

★ ★ ★

In the mind of Ver, advised by his coterie of favorite generals, the by-the-books solution to a stubborn, immovable crowd is a CDC (Crowd Dispersal and Control Unit). On that fateful Saturday, all CDCs including that of Camp Crame's, were under the operational control of Ver. These were CDCs from Malacañang, the Army, Air Force, Navy, Constabulary, and the Police.

Lulled by his earlier "success" in crushing the coup, and assured that the Presidential Security Command could protect Malacañang, Ver, like his Commander-in-Chief, believed the situation was under control.

Three things obviously did not figure in the mind of Ver, or if they did, he simply minimized their importance.

The first was that he had tied his hands with the agreement to freeze all troop movements, which was approved and announced by Marcos on TV.

Secondly, even if he wanted to disregard the military freeze and proceed to disperse the swelling throng around the camps, not all his CDCs could cope with the removal of some fifty thousand people. All told, his CDCs numbered not more than 7,000. And even if Ver had ordered all CDCs to move in, more than half of them would have ignored him, specially the better trained Constabulary and Police CDCs.

Thirdly, there was the attitude of the crowd. The people at Camp Aguinaldo and Camp Crame appeared prepared to die rather than yield ground. Such an attitude, bordering on fanaticism, may be attributed to an intense hatred for Marcos and his wife, and the dramatic, timely appearance of Enrile and Ramos as champions of their cause.

No other symbol of deliverance could have elicited the same spontaneous demonstrations of the Filipino cooperative spirit, or *bayanihan*.

★ ★ ★

Over at Malacañang, Marcos who perhaps appreciated more than Ver the tactical significance of the presence of the crowd at Camp Aguinaldo and Camp Crame, was wondering why the crowd had not been dispersed. That job primarily belonged to the Police, and as reserves, to the Constabulary.

Maj. Gen. Prospero A. Olivas, who commanded the PC Metrocom and the Metropolitan Police Force, recounts in the following narrative how insistent Marcos was for the Aguinaldo-Crame crowds to be dispersed and how the general pretended to carry out the order.

"On Saturday evening (February 22), the President called me up to say that he was designating me as acting chief of Constabulary and director general of the Integrated National Police (replacing Ramos). He directed me to disperse the crowds at the vicinity of Camp Aguinaldo and Camp Crame immediately so that an attack could be launched against Minister Enrile and General Ramos with tanks, mortar, and even artillery. But I did not conduct any crowd control and dispersal operations that night and waited for "people power" to grow in large numbers, so that Minister Enrile and General Ramos would be safe.

"However, I made Malacañang believe that I was going to disperse the crowd. I was stalling for time.

"I was asked again by the President whether I had started dispersal operations. I reasoned out that we were still gathering our men. However, I assured him that we would be acting soon.

"He called again later to inquire whether we were ready to disperse the crowd. I said my men were ready and were just waiting for the trucks which Brig. Gen. Felix Brawner, Jr. promised to dispatch to transport my men.

"The President called again. He sounded impatient because we had not dispersed the crowd yet. I assured him we would be dispersing the crowd soon but we would have to commandeer vehicles to transport our men.

"All my moves were intended to make Malacañang depend on me rather than on other troops from the Army, Air Force, and Navy to disperse the people. Our standard operating procedure was for military units to assist us only when we requested reinforcements.

"The President called up again and asked if the crowd had already been dispersed. I replied that the crowd was so big that it was beyond the capability of my men to disperse it. He ordered me to get in touch with Maj. Gen. Josephus Ramas, commander of the Army, and ask for reinforcements. I did not contact General Ramas. Thus, no crowd control operation was conducted on Saturday night."

★ ★ ★

Olivas' switch to Enrile-Ramos had come easily, almost effortlessly, as indicated by the following telephone conversation just after Enrile and Ramos declared their break with Marcos:

General Ramos — Olive, you know the score, and we are counting on your support.

General Olivas — Yes, Sir.

★ ★ ★

Olivas' defection was not known to Malacañang. He had been waiting for Ramos at Camp Crame when he was stricken ill. His blood pressure was 160/110 and his pulse rate, 130 per minute. The doctors ordered him taken to nearby Camp Panopio for treatment. It was there that Ramos reached him by phone. Olivas was later transferred to the Constabulary Station Hospital at Camp Crame and then, because he was very ill, General Ramos arranged his transfer to the Philippine Heart Center for Asia the following day.

During the night in broadcasts made by Ramos to announce the defections to the rebel side, Olivas was not mentioned. The idea was to keep Malacañang believing in Olivas' loyalty and giving him orders which Olivas would pass on to Ramos.

★ ★ ★

Like Marcos, Ver believed that General Olivas was still loyal. ISAFP had failed to carry out his order to destroy Radio Veritas. He thought of Olivas for the job. It was at 11 p.m. while Marcos was having a press conference that Ver reached the ailing Olivas by phone. He ordered him to silence Radio Veritas because it was inciting large crowds to Camp Aguinaldo and Camp Crame.

Olivas replied, "Yes, Sir."

But Olivas did not take action.

A few minutes later, Minister Juan Tuvera, the presidential executive assistant, called Olivas to remind him that it was Marcos' desire that Radio Veritas be "neutralized" and that the order must be carried out immediately. Olivas, keeping up the charade, assured him the order would be carried out.

★ ★ ★

Through the night, Ver searched his brain for a path to victory, and thought of plunging the Enrile-Ramos camp in darkness by cutting off their electrical power supply. It would kill the second bird with the same stone as it would deny power to Radio Veritas which was just a couple of kilometers to the north. So Ver ordered Brig. Gen. Feliciano Suarez, chief of the 52nd Engineer Brigade, to switch off the two camps from the power line. But as the supplier of electricity was the Manila Electric Company (Meralco), Suarez had to transmit Ver's order to retired Brig. Gen. Francisco Gatmaitan of that company.

"No way," Gatmaitan replied. Did not Ver realize that a blackout would deny power to the Philippine Heart Center for Asia where Marcos' mother, Doña Josefa, was confined for a heart condition? Adversely affected, too, would be the V. Luna Medical Center, the main military hospital, and at least a dozen other government and private hospitals.

Suarez told Ver of the consequences of such an "inhuman" act. Ver had another idea: cut off the water connections. Suarez came back with a similar argument. Ver gave up.

As the night dragged on at the Ministry of National Defense building, Enrile received visitors who came with assurances of their support. Among the callers was Butz Aquino, who had a private conversation with Enrile. Mass was said by Fr. Bert Clemeña, a Catholic priest who in the early days of Enrile's ministry was a reporter covering the defense and military beat.

★ ★ ★

Midnight fell on the nation in the throes of a revolution. The Enrile-Ramos rebellion was only five and a half hours old, but for the two gallant men, there was no turning back . . . The die was cast, or as Enrile put it in his own words:

"We have already broken the shell of the egg. There is nothing left to do but to stir it." □

CHAPTER II

DAY 2

February 23, 1986

He who hesitates is lost.

— Proverb

Unus homo nobis cunctando restituit rem.
(One man by delaying, saved the state for us.)

— Ennius, De Senectate, IV:10

FROM VACILLATION TO IMPOTENCE

Marcos must have spent a sleepless night, torn between the desire to crush the Enrile-Ramos revolt and the need to avoid the condemnation that history would heap on him for the slaughter. This was a Sunday, and Marcos was a meditative man.

His generals did not have any sleep at all. After a huddle with Ver at the Tactical Operations Center at Malacañang Park when the Enrile-Ramos breakaway was known, they met again at the same place at 3 a.m., and agreed to use military might to bring the rebels to their knees. Ver picked Ramas, the head of the Army, to be in command of the operations.

Ramas called for a planning conference at 5 a.m. at the Army headquarters at Fort Bonifacio, about 10 kilometers to the southeast. Present were Major Gen. Vicente Piccio, Air Force commander; Rear Adm. Brillante Ochoco, Navy commander; Brig. Gen. Felix Brawner, operations commander and concurrent chief of the First Scout Ranger Regiment; Commodore Serapio Martillano; Brig. Gen. Feliciano Suarez, 52nd Engineer Brigade commander; and Brig. Gen. Angel Sadang. Brig. Gen. Isidoro de Guzman, RUC 3 (Central Luzon) commander, excused himself from the meeting.

This was the scheme drawn up by the conferees: Marines would be the main strike force; Army troopers would be held in reserve; Air Force and Naval units would provide general support.

Fort Bonifacio was the staging area for the action, so Tadiar pulled out the 3rd and the 5th Marine Battalion Landing Teams from Malacañang and assembled them at the Fort. The 14th Infantry Battalion was to establish checkpoints at all points of entry east of Metro Manila.

In compliance with Marcos' wish that Enrile and Ramos be denied escape by air, Ver ordered Singson to have his people destroy the two helicopters parked behind the ministry building. The choppers had brought in arms and ammunition for the rebels the day before. Obviously, Ver did not know that Singson and the entire ISAFP had shifted their loyalty to Enrile. Singson told Ver it was impossible to blow up the helicopters because a single explosion, even from gunfire, would provoke hostile reaction that could lead to the "bloody mess" that Marcos wanted to avoid. Balbanero seconded the motion. The order was not carried out. As a safety measure, Piccio ordered his people at Clark and Subic to keep an eye on any ministry helicopter and arrest its passengers if it landed.

★ ★ ★

Throughout the day, Ver called for reinforcements from Brig. Gen. Tomas Dumpit of Regional Unified Command (RUC) 1, Col. Milton Tiburcio of RUC 12, Brig. Gen. Madrino Muñoz of RUC-10, and Col. Marcos Betacura also of RUC-12. He also wired Lt. Col. Reynaldo Berroya to change his mind about shifting support to Enrile and Ramos.

★ ★ ★

Before the break of dawn, listeners felt something amiss: Radio Veritas, their only link to the action unfolding at Camp Aguinaldo, had gone off the air. The voice of the Catholic Church had been silenced, its powerful transmission facilities in Bulacan, north of Manila, wrecked by about 30 unidentified armed men who came in 10 cars and over-powered and disarmed its two guards. June Keithley, who had been anchoring the newscasts, ran to Manila to arrange for an alternate station, possibly DZRH. She was turned down. Fr. James Reuter, S.J., advised Keithley to go home and wait for developments. Soon Reformist officers came to see her and told her she could use a clandestine station, to be known as "Radyo ng Bayan" (People's Radio). Actually "DZRB" was DZRJ, with its booth located about two kilometers east of Malacañang. The place had been secured for Keithley. A clever technician made a few modifications to enable listeners tuned in to Veritas to pick up Keithley's broadcasts, which continually carried messages from Enrile and Ramos.

★ ★ ★

General Olivas was thus spared the odius task of destroying Veritas. But the crowd dispersal order still hung over the head of the Metrocom commander. Early in the morning, he got a call from Malacañang to report at 11 a.m. and take his oath of office before Marcos as chief of Constabulary and director general of the Integrated National Police. But his blood pressure had risen during the night and he had to be placed under oxygen and given medication. Recalling that incident now, Olivas calls his ailment as a godsend.

★ ★ ★

From Ver to Ramas to Brawner to Police Brig. Gen. Alfredo Lim of the Northern Police District came the command to disperse the crowd which had dwindled to about 3,000 and clear the way for the attacking force. Brawner dispatched a 265-man CDC unit of the Army to beef up

Lim's 118 men. When the Army unit arrived at Camp Panopio from Cubao, Lim told its commander that he did not need them. The soldiers went back to Fort Bonifacio.

Impatient over the lack of action against the crowd, Ver sent Malacañang CDC elements to Libis, behind the ministry building, and to Bonny Serrano avenue which bounded Camps Aguinaldo and Crame on the northeast. By this time the crowd had swelled again to almost 50,000 and was increasing by the minute. The Malacañang unit picked up some policemen from the Southern Police District to augment its force. Their crowd dispersal attempt was a failure.

Meanwhile, Piccio sent up an aerial photo team to take pictures of the situation at the Aguinaldo-Crame area. The team spotted a weak link in the "people power" chain around the camps: Libis. To crash through this vulnerable link, Piccio assigned two armed S-76 helicopters to support the Marines.

This soft spot was a mere hundred meters from where Enrile and his friends heard Holy Mass at the ministry building that Sunday morning. Ramos came over for the rites, after which he told Enrile that he should join him at Camp Crame. Then the general returned to Crame, and was wildly cheered by the crowd along the way. He was his usual calm, confident self.

★   ★   ★

Back at the Palace, Ver was moving the pawns on his military chessboard. He ordered an infantry battalion in Zamboanga to fly to Manila and report to Fort Bonifacio. The 14th Infantry Battalion to proceed to Libis. The 8th Marine Battalion Landing Team in Bataan, he ordered to move to Fort Bonifacio, and Ochoco dispatched a ship to transport the unit.

For his part, Ramos did not have to order any troop movements. They just happened — entire military commands moving to the side of what he now called the New Armed Forces of the Philippines. A stream of telegrams and courier-borne messages piled up on his desk as he planned the defense of the Aguinaldo-Crame perimeter.

★ ★ ★

An unbelieving and nervous Col. Alexander P. Aguirre, chief of operations at Constabulary headquarters, arrived from Baguio City at 4:30 a.m. Aguirre was stunned by the news aired over Radio Veritas that Enrile and his chief had parted ways with Marcos and Ver . . . but Camp Crame was absolutely without any defenses for such a contingency! So he rushed to Ramos' side and worked continuously on the defense plan in line with these guidelines laid down by Ramos:

1. Galvanize and make maximum use of "people power".

2. Undertake no provocative military action against the opposing side.

This was the first time in Philippine military history that "people power" was mentioned in a defense plan. A group of people massed to obstruct military movements had become an element of military strategy and tactics. Something new for the books. The closest relative of "people power" that a student of history can think of was how the Germans during the last world war shelled Polish villages on the path of oncoming Polish military units in order to create a traffic jam out of fleeing civilians and block the advancing Polish soldiers. But the Philippine situation is different in that the people played their role as human obstacles on purpose.

Months before the revolution, the Reformists were already aware of what the people, properly harnessed, could do to help them cleanse the armed forces. In their campaign to pressure Marcos to attend to the deterioration of the armed forces, the group assigned Army Col. Jose Almonte and Navy Capt. Felix Turingan to enlist the sympathy of mass and professional organizations for the Movement. To be sure, the hundreds of people with whom Turingan and Almonte had talked to turned out to be part of the human walls around Aguinaldo and Crame.

Aguirre, with the help of Col. Ismael Villareal, established an operations center to work closely with the command center of Ramos in the same Constabulary headquarters building in Camp Crame. For Aguirre, defense in depth was militarily unattainable because the camp was too small and there were not enough troops. "But a defense in depth was made possible with "people power," Aguirre said. "The area of Camp Crame constituting just one small block had extended its boundaries: to the south along Ortigas avenue; to the Ortigas-Santolan-Mariposa streets in the west; to Libis in the east; and to P. Tuazon-EDSA in the north by means of the human barricades of "people power."

It became possible for the Crame operations center to activate the following blockading actions:

1. Creation of traffic jams or "choke points" along EDSA, the Sta. Mesa area and the approaches from the Pasig River side;

2. Blockade of the North Diversion road and approaches from Bulacan with the use of Metro Manila Transport Corporation buses and people barricades to prevent troop reinforcements from the north;

3. Blowing up of exit roads from Camp Capinpin undertaken by the Rizal Constabulary to prevent reinforcements from Marcos-Ver troops coming from the town of Tanay in the east;

4. People barricades at Horseshoe-Santolan roads to blockade Crame's rear; and

5. Mobilization of "people power" to create diversionary demonstrations at Mendiola and Nagtahan, especially on the night of February 25, the day of Marcos' oathtaking, to prevent troop movement from Malacañang toward Crame and television station MBS 4.

That was the defense plan, but no one claimed that it would make Aguinaldo and Crame impregnable to a massive ground and air assault. The defense in depth woven out of "people power" rested on the assumption that the human barricades would be respected by the attacking forces or that these obstacles would be strong enough to resist men in their machines. It was a gamble, a calculated risk, but General Ramos had indomitable faith that "God will always be on the side of the good." Aguirre had himself admitted that "Crame may have a determined stand, but against a determined and heartless assault, it will simply be overwhelmed," a perception shared by Enrile and Ramos, though they kept it from the public.

★ ★ ★

At Fort Bonifacio that Sunday morning, Army Commander Ramas moved to devise the military juggernaut to crush the rebels. At 9 a.m. he called another planning conference and put together two Provisional Tactical Brigades out of the First Marine Provisional Division (FMPD), each having two battalions, and an armored company, in line with plans drawn up by Brawner.

The FMPD was placed under the command of Brig. Gen. Jose Paez, the 1st PTB under Col. Braulio Balbas, the 2nd PTB under Col. Eugenio Reyes, and the armor under Major Sergio Eria.

The idea was that after the crowd would have been swept away by CDC units in Libis, the regiment under Balbas would enter Camp Aguinaldo through the Logistics Command area, take possession of Camp Aguinaldo, then position tanks and mortar for the bombardment of Camp Crame, after which Marines would pour into Camp Crame, occupy it and take captives. Reyes' regiment would come into the fray in case Balbas' men could not finish the job. Crame would also be under artillery fire from howitzers positioned at the University of Life about three kilometers southeast of Crame.

More troops were moved into Manila. Two companies of the 8th Marine Battalion were told to move in from Bataan, but only after making sure that there was no threat of attack from Communist New People's Army elements there.

At 11 a.m., the Ramas juggernaut was poised for the slam on the beleaguered camps. But Ver and all the other generals left Ramas at Fort Bonifacio while they rushed to Malacañang to stand behind Marcos during a televised press conference.

★ ★ ★

The scenery at Malacañang had become more metallic: the grounds were bristling with armor. Two tanks were in front of the administration building, three in front of the Maharlika Hall, and three more at odd places.

Reporters began to stream into the Ceremonial Hall for the press conference. There were foreign correspondents and international networks people. At a corner of the hall, the First Lady talked to some Filipino newsmen. One of them remembered her saying, "*Masyadong mabait lang kasi ang Sir ninyo. Noong 1972 ko pa sinabi sa kanya, 'Baka si Johnny na iyan ang papatay sa iyo,' Tingnan ninyo ngayon.*" ("Your Sir has been inordinately lenient. As far back as 1972, I had already told him, 'Watch out, it might be Johnny who will kill you,' Now, look what's happened!")

The presence of Cabinet members and other top government and military officials was meant to demonstrate that the government was intact and the armed forces still loyal to Marcos. At the presidential table were Presidential Executive Assistant Juan C. Tuvera, Agrarian Reform Minister Conrado Estrella, Public Works Minister Jesus Hipolito, Food Administrator Jesus Tanchangco, Agriculture Minister Salvador Escudero III, Education Minister Jaime C. Laya, Member of Parliament Teodulo Natividad, Political Affairs Minister Leonardo Perez, Budget Minister Manuel Alba, MP Salvador Britanico, former acting Foreign Minister Pacifico Castro, Manila International Airport Manager Luis Tabuena, Isabela Governor Faustino Dy, Information Minister Gregorio Cendaña, Justice Minister Estelito Mendoza, Justice Buenaventura Guerrero, Assistant Press Secretary Amante Bigornia, MP Antonio Raquiza, Economic Planning Minister Vicente Valdepeñas, and former Senator Rodolfo Ganzon.

Standing behind them were General Ver, Rear Adm. Brillante Ochoco, and lesser stars Felix Brawner, Carlos Martel, Juanito Veridiano, Hamilton Dimaya, Eustaquio Purugganan, Telesforo Tayko, Serapio Martillano, Pompeyo Vasquez, Victorino Azada, Arsenio Silva, Evaristo Sanchez, Emerson Tangan, and Navy Captain Danilo Lazo. (The following day, one of them moved over to Camp Crame.)

They had to wait for a while because Marcos was in another room talking to Captain Morales, Major Aromin, and two more — Lt. Col. Jake Malajacan and Major Ricardo Brillantes — who had not as yet made statements on TV confessing their part in a reported plot on the lives of the First Couple and a coup engineered by the Reformists.

Marcos then walked into the Ceremonial Hall. The four detained officers were brought in, in two's, by Diego, the PSC lawyer. Ver glared at the captives as the four men took seats to the President's left. Marcos presented them, and said there were others who had been arrested but were still being interrogated.

It was evident that the objective was to downgrade the emerging popularity of Enrile and Ramos who, he insisted, were participants in the aborted coup and assassination. Marcos' advisers had been vocal in their opinion that Malacañang was losing the battle for the hearts and minds of the citizens. The presentation of more participants in the aborted coup would hopefully give a boost to Malacañang credibility.

Malajacan read his statement and Brillantes his affidavit.

Marcos was sure as ever that the situation was under control: "It is not true that the armed forces is divided into equal factions. Barring those who are now with Enrile and Ramos. I don't believe there are other officers willing to be included in the list of the rebellion or identified with the coup."

Marcos said Ver was meeting with all important military commanders and that Brig. Gen. Jose Magno in Mindanao and Brig. Gen. Alexander Felix in Isabela were loyal to him, contrary to reports. The meeting never materialized, however.

Aguinaldo and Crame, Marcos continued, were already surrounded by Ver's forces. The troops around Camp Aguinaldo were under General Piccio and Brig. Gen. Luther Custodio of the AVSECOM. They have two battalions of PAF security, he reported.

He added, "Tadiar of the Marines is commanding troops around the camps. Some troops are around the Corinthian Gardens adjacent to Aguinaldo."

But Marcos said he had ordered the troops surrounding the camps to "be patient and not start the hostilities." (The truth was that the troops were not really surrounding their objectives; there were none to the west, north, and east. Marcos must have been given a wrong situation map.)

Marcos warned Enrile and Ramos: "Let the blood of those who will die be on your conscience." Later, he relented: "The options are with us. We could finish this in one hour but it would be a bloody mess and I don't want that."

Marcos said he was not sick and if Enrile and Ramos would not yield, he would personally lead the troops and wipe them out. He described himself as an old war horse chafing at the bit after smelling gunpowder. He said it was easy to attack Camp Crame. "The first thing you must do is cordon off the area from civilians." (This prompted more people power participants to augment the Camp Crame barricades and mass as far as Ortigas and Guadalupe, according to reconnaisance by Tadiar's forces.)

With the big stick firmly in his right hand, Marcos held up the olive branch to Enrile and Ramos with another invitation to negotiate.

Marcos complained: "I was willing to converse with him (Enrile) on the telephone but he suddenly clammed up when I told him they (Enrile and Ramos) would have to face trial, that they would have to confront witnesses against them in legal proceedings."

A reporter asked if he had set a deadline for Enrile and Ramos to begin and end negotiations.

"Deadline? That, I leave to the military. But I'm trying my best to get in touch with Johnny Ponce Enrile, so we can use intermediaries one of whom they approved . . . retired Lt. Gen. Rafael Ileto, ambassador to Thailand.

"I am not giving up my position of non-hostile resolution of this matter. I will exert all efforts to bring this to a non-bloody end," Marcos replied.

Asked if he was about to resign, Marcos affirmed strongly, "I am not about to resign, of course not, of course not!"

It was 2 p.m. when the press conference broke up and Marcos called his Cabinet to a meeting which was to take the better part of one hour.

★   ★   ★

The arrest of Malajacan and Aromin caused Brig. Gen. Roland Pattugalan, 2nd Division commander and a relative of Marcos, to summon the brigade commander, Col. Alejandro A. Galido. Galido came all the way from Quezon province east of Manila to report to Pattugalan at Fort Bonifacio at 3 p.m. on the alleged assassination plot. Pattugalan berated Galido for not reporting the activities of the two battalion commanders, and ordered him to take custody of Malajacan and Aromin. He could not communicate with his family. In other words, he was "neutralized," spawning a wave of dissent among the people in his brigade. Later, Pattugalan ordered Galido to move his brigade to Manila.

After the press conference, Ver got wind of morale problems in the Army, Air Force, and Marines. He went to Fort Bonifacio together with Ochoco, Bello, Corrachea, Brawner, and Col. Ver to give the boys a pep talk. On the advice of his son, Irwin, Ver took along detainees Morales, Aromin, Malajacan, and Brillantes to display them as proof that the reported assassination plot was for real.

In the middle of Ver's speech, Brawner left to rush to his Scout Ranger regiment where there was also a morale problem involving about 20 Philippine Military Academy (PMA) alumni among the officers whose hearts were with the Reformists. Brawner promised them reforms and asked for time to implement them. Just the same, Lt. Noel Buan turned over his firearm and said he was leaving his unit to join Enrile and Ramos. He was prevailed upon to wait another day.

From Fort Bonifacio, Ver and his party proceeded to Villamor Air Base at 5 p.m. where a similar pep talk and exhibition of the detainees was made. At 7 p.m., Ver was called to the Maharlika Lounge where the Papal Nuncio, Monsignor Bruno Torpigliani, Ricardo Cardinal Vidal, and Monsignor Severino Pelayo were waiting for him. The nuncio had a letter for Marcos from Pope John Paul II appealing for a peaceful settlement of the issue. Jaime Cardinal Sin was not with the party because hit men were reportedly out to get him.

★ ★ ★

As Marcos wound up his press conference, Enrile prepared to vacate the ministry building at Camp Aguinaldo and move over to Constabulary headquarters at Camp Crame. At 2:24 p.m. Enrile was on his way to the EDSA on foot, followed by the "Cagayan 100" contingent and his security group. A number of security men were in a convoy of trucks. As he reached the gate, he was lustily cheered by the crowd of men, women, and children. The air was rent with the gleeful chant of "Johnny, Johnny, Johnny!"

A witness recalled that the sea of humanity on EDSA parted like the Red Sea of Biblical times to make way for Enrile's party to cross smoothly to the Crame gate and move on to the four-story Constabulary headquarters building. He met Ramos at the penthouse, from which they greeted the crowd on EDSA. Again the applause was a roar of delight and approval. In the next couple of days, Enrile and Ramos would join the crowd below in the Holy Masses and in impromptu entertainment shows put up by movie and TV personalities as a means to release tension and relieve fatigue.

From that penthouse, too, Enrile and Ramos were to view the oncoming forces of Tadiar.

Enrile left behind at Camp Aguinaldo a small group of soldiers, clerks, and some officers of ISAFP who had declared their loyalty to the rebels. The main body moved to the ISAFP installation in Bago Bantay district about six kilometers to the north. The stay-behind group was led by Estrellado. Singson was in Bago Bantay. In Camp Aguinaldo, the "neutral" force of Balbanero was weakened when one company of MPs marched to Crame with Enrile.

★ ★ ★

At Fort Bonifacio, there was no immediate response to Ver's command given from Malacañang at 1:30 p.m. that the "intimidation" force jump off towards Aguinaldo and Crame. Ver's idea was for the axe to fall while Marcos was telling Enrile and Ramos over television to yield. Planner of the operation was Tadiar. Here is how the force was organized (a modification of plans made in the morning): the intimidator was called the first Marine Provisional Division with Brig. Gen. Jose Paez as commanding general. The division had two brigades: the 4th Marine Provisional Brigade led by Col. Braulio Balbas, Jr. and the 5th Marine Provisional Brigade led by Col. Eugenio Reyes. Each brigade had two battalions. The 4th Brigade was to assault and seize the Constabulary headquarters building in Camp Crame.

With Ramas at Fort Bonifacio was a battle staff composed of Generals Angel Kanapi, Ramon Cannu, Cirilo Oropesa, Brawner, and Colonel Abadilla. Among the visitors who came to see how the coercive operations were going were Piccio, Ochoco, Custodio, Corrachea, Bello, Palafox, Alcantara, and MP Orlando Dulay.

It was almost 2 p.m. when Ramas prodded Tadiar to get the Marine column moving toward the camps. Tadiar replied he was still waiting for the last batches of Marines he had pulled out of Malacañang to come into Fort Bonifacio. Ramas warned Tadiar to move on the double as the original order was from Marcos. Ramas knew fully well that Marcos wanted the troops to move into position without bloodshed and that there would be no firing until and unless Marcos ordered it himself.

At 2:15 p.m., the 1st Marine Provisional Division finally jumped off from Fort Bonifacio with Tadiar in the lead vehicle instead of Paez. It was a formidable column spearheaded by armor. Witnesses counted 6 tanks, 10 armored personnel carriers, 8 jeeps, and 13 six-by-six trucks. The column rolled through Forbes road and turned right into EDSA. Before it reached Ortigas avenue, which was about a kilometer from Crame and Aguinaldo, it came to a halt.

The road was filled with people, some of them lying down, daring the tanks to crush them. Others were praying and singing religious songs. Nuns and priests were everywhere. People were appealing to the Marines not to go one step further. The Marines decided to bypass the human sea, turned right before reaching Ortigas and crashed through a cement wall into a vacant lot aiming to exit at a portion of Ortigas, but the exit was again blocked by onrushing masses of people. Tadiar tried to open a dialogue with the people. There were opposition and church leaders among them. The reply was the same: "Turn back!"

Ramos sent the same appeal to Tadiar. Enrile telephoned Marcos to order the tanks away. On a suggestion of Marcos that the entire rebel group surrender, Enrile said he needed time to consult with Ramos and Honasan, whom Marcos identified as the leader of the attempt to assassinate the First Couple. Marcos assured Enrile he would order the tank commanders not to fire but said he could not prevent them from taking up assigned positions.

While the Marines were at a standstill and the officers were at a loss on what to do, Ramas radioed orders to Tadiar to move ahead to the objective areas. Tadiar described to him the situation. "I don't want to hurt these people," Tadiar told the Army chief. "I'm also human like you."

Kanapi and Col. Lisandro Abadia, the Army operations officer, came by helicopter and conferred with Tadiar. Tadiar recommended an aerial reconnaisance, so the three of them boarded the helicopter and viewed the Aguinaldo-Crame area and its environs. Kanapi pointed to several possible routes of approach, but Tadiar asked him to consider how the human barricades were thickening by the minute. It had not been an hour since the last Crame radio appeal for more of "people power."

Upon their return to the Ortigas lot where the Marines were bogged down, Tadiar began to think about the best approach among those Kanapi suggested: take the road to the right of the Corinthian Gardens, then proceed to Gate 5 of Camp Aguinaldo. But the risk of hurting civilians had not been removed and Tadiar dismissed the idea.

Kanapi and Abadia flew back to Ramas but after a while Abadia was back to convey Ramas' instructions to Tadiar. Two Marine battalions were to be "injected" into Camp Aguinaldo while the armored units and other elements of the division were to be sent back to Fort Bonifacio. Balbas' battalions were picked for the Aguinaldo mission. The rest of the division went home at 4:20 p.m.

This was how Tadiar summed up Balbas' 3rd and 5th Marine Battalions' "injection" effort: "On or about 2000h (8 p.m.) Col. Balbas reported to me that his unit was stopped by human barricades at Libis and there was no way they could penetrate without hurting innocent civilians. He further reported that all possible approaches to Camp Aguinaldo were full of people. I therefore ordered him to return to Fort Bonifacio."

Ramas and his associates were busy up to midnight devising another way to capture the Aguinaldo-Crame area. A big help was Brig. Gen. Victor Natividad, who had replaced the ailing Olivas as head of the Metropolitan command. Natividad showed how the stubborn human barricades could be breached.

★   ★   ★

About the time the Marines were bogged down on Ortigas avenue, another drama was taking place at the Manila International Airport. A hijacked Philippine Air Lines BAC 111 from Cotabato, one of the southernmost Philippine provinces, landed at the Manila International Airport at 3:25 p.m. The Aviation Security Command had been forwarned about the hijack and upon arrival of the plane, all the hijackers were arrested. The people who had seized the plane in Cotabato were Maj. Billy Bibit and 4 other officers, one police officer and 97 soldiers enroute to join Enrile and Ramos at Camp Crame. With the guns of about 100 men and two V-150s trained on them as they emerged from the plane they had no option but to give up. They were disarmed and taken to a detention facility at Fort Bonifacio then aboard two Philippine Navy vessels for billeting purposes, and finally back to Fort Bonifacio where they sat out the revolution.

★   ★   ★

Camp Crame's experience with the aborted attack caused greater defensive measures to be instituted. More time had to be gained for the continued shift of armed forces loyalty to Enrile-Ramos. Airpower was badly needed for both defensive and offensive actions. There were only two choppers on their side, the ones that on Saturday were hidden behind the Ministry building and which Ver had repeatedly ordered destroyed. The behavior of people power under actual stress from the military standpoint having been observed, it was thought that more of it should be mobilized, with instructions and guidance provided the people for their safety and maximum effectiveness.

★ ★ ★

Earlier that morning of Day 2, the Enrile-Ramos camp decided to press its psychological advantage in the fight for the loyalty of the troops. The call of Enrile and Ramos for AFP units and individual officers and men to move over to the rebel side, aired on radio, had elicited heartwarming response. But there was need to follow it through with a written appeal. So a text was prepared at 9:30 that morning by Brig. Gen. Eduardo Ermita, Col. Honesto Isleta, and retired Col. Noe Andaya, and dictated by phone by Col. Ruben Ciron to a friendly printing press which had 50,000 copies ready by afternoon. A PC Bolkow helicopter picked up the leaflets at the Quezon City Memorial Circle and dropped them at the known encampments of Marcos loyalist troops in Cubao, Camp Aguinaldo, Ortigas, Fort Bonifacio, and Villamor Air Base.

The appeal, titled "A Call to All Officers and Men of the AFP and the INP," read:

> "WE ARE CALLING ALL OFFICERS AND MEN OF THE AFP AND THE INP TO EXAMINE THEIR CONSCIENCE AND BE GUIDED BY THEIR CONVICTION.
>
> "IF THEY BELIEVE IN WHAT THEY STAND FOR, WE ASK THEM TO JOIN US. WE ASK THEM TO BRING THEIR TROOPS WITH THEM AND JOIN US HERE IN CAMP AGUINALDO OR CAMP CRAME AND IF THEY SHOULD DECIDE OTHERWISE, WE ASK THEM TO STAY PUT AND NOT OBEY ILLEGAL AND IMMORAL ORDERS."
>
> — FROM ALL THE THOUSANDS OF OFFICERS AND MEN COMMITTED TO FIGHT FOR TRUTH, RIGHTEOUSNESS AND JUSTICE AND ARE NOW GATHERED AT CAMP AGUINALDO AND CAMP CRAME."

As with the radio appeal, the response was tremendous.

★ ★ ★

In the evening, Enrile and Ramos stepped up the effort to gain ground in the psychological phase of their do-or-die venture. At 7 p.m. they called a press conference and here Ramos went on to enumerate the military commanders and units that had abandoned Marcos and come over to the rebel side. It was a long list which included even those claimed by Marcos earlier in the day to be loyal to Malacañang. The list was a lengthening litany of defections from Marcos all over the country: Luzon, the Visayas, and Mindanao.

Ramos said 61 Constabulary provincial commanders and 7 metropolitan district commanders had radioed their defection. In Region I (which includes the home province of Marcos), Abra and Pangasinan had turned their backs on Marcos. Brig. Gen. Thomas Manlongat's Region II covering the Cagayan Valley; the provincial commands of Nueva Ecija, Pampanga, and Bataan and the metropolitan district commands of Angeles City and Olongapo City in Region III (Central Luzon) had shed their loyalty to Marcos. So had the provincial commands of Rizal and Batangas in Southern Luzon; the entire Region V command in the Bicol area; the whole regional command of Region VI (Western Visayas); the whole regional command of Region VIII (Eastern Visayas); the provincial commands of Negros Occidental, Siquijor, Bohol, and Cebu and the metropolitan district command of Cebu City in Region VII (Central Visayas); and the entire Constabulary commands of Regions IX, X, XI, and XII (Mindanao).

The Association of General and Flag Officers (AGFO) headed by Brig. Gen. Mariano Ordoñez and veterans of the Philippine Expeditionary Forces to Korea (PEFTOK) also rallied to the cause of Enrile and Ramos.

No longer on Marcos' side was the 950th Air Wing, which is the communications and electronics wing commanded by Col. Camello Beltran, and the three police superintendents in Metro Manila, Brig. Gen. Narciso Cabrera, Brig. Gen. Alfredo Yson, and Brig. Gen. Alfredo Lim. This fact alone should explain why Marcos could not depend on the crowd dispersal and control units of the Police.

The defections within the armed forces were developing with a bandwagon effect. The momentum was to continue in the next two days and would be disastrous to Marcos and Ver. Indeed, time was now in the rebels' favor.

★ ★ ★

With the pendulum of the armed forces swinging away from Marcos, Enrile began to take a tougher stance. In the evening, he received MP Alfonso Reyno of Cagayan and MP Rodolfo Albano of Isabela. To Reyno who was insisting that he talk with Marcos, Enrile said, "Look Boy (Reyno), I cannot talk to the President. What will I say? I cannot negotiate with him. I cannot surrender. Now then, you please tell him that we are totally committed to this and there is no way to change our position."

"Well, he just wants to talk to you."

"What for?" Enrile asked.

Realizing that Enrile could not be persuaded to change his mind, Reyno pleaded that Enrile just talk with Marcos over the telephone. Enrile agreed. A portion of the conversation follows:

Marcos — Johnny, I am not going to harm your men. All I want is for the group of Colonel Honasan to go through a pro forma trial so that we can show that we are enforcing the law. And I assure you that I will give them a pardon.

Enrile — Mr. President, I don't think they have committed any crime. Why should they surrender? Anyway, I will explain to them and I will come back to you. You see, I cannot decide this because we now have a committee on a one-man-one-vote basis.

So, according to Enrile, he kept Marcos waiting for the decision on the surrender of the Reformists. He also kept Marcos' emissaries comfortable while waiting for the decision. After some time, Enrile told Reyno and Albano: "Will you please go to the President and carry a message to him that the situation has changed, that it is already a problem involving the interest of the people, and the bottom line demand — which is non-negotiable — is for him to step down!"

The two MPs were stunned. The rebellion had grown into a full-blown revolution.

★ ★ ★

Marcos was furious when he got the message.

That night, Malacañang reporters were surprised to be notified of another press conference.

Marcos said it had become clear that Enrile had knowledge of the aborted coup and the plot to assassinate him and the First Lady. "There is evidence now that from the very beginning, Enrile was out to grab power and rule the country through a junta. Enrile would become the chairman of the council that would take over the government. The council would be composed of representatives of different sectors such as the clergy which would most probably be represented by Cardinal Sin, the opposition represented by Mrs. Aquino, the military represented by General Ramos, and a representative of the business sector. Mrs. Aquino should not delude herself into thinking that she is being supported by Enrile because she would be a mere member of the junta."

Of Cardinal Sin, Marcos said, "He is an inciter to rebellion and a mouther of subversive and rebellious statements. I will attend to him later."

Marcos dismissed the claim of growing support for Enrile and Ramos. "The armed forces are behind the President," he stressed. "I will not put much weight on reports that several provincial commanders have expressed support for them." He asked how they could claim the support of the provincial commanders of La Union and Pangasinan when these officers had already pledged their loyalty to the President.

The report on the capture of Major Bibit and the men who had hijacked the PAL plane was cited by Marcos as evidence of the futility of provincial support for the revolutionary movement.

Marcos said Enrile, Ramos, and the Reformists with them would have to face trial for rebellion, and their occupancy of the Constabulary headquarters building was illegal because they were no longer officials of the government.

Marcos reiterated that he would not step down from office "on the mere say-so of those who criticize my administration."

★ ★ ★

In Cebu City on this Sunday, Mrs. Aquino decided to fly back to Manila instead of going on to Davao City to continue her campaign for civil disobedience. Her running mate, Salvador Laurel, two of her advisers, Teodoro Locsin and Rene Saguisag, and the venerable opposition leader, 87-year-old Lorenzo Tañada, were among the callers at Camp Crame. Laurel congratulated Enrile and Ramos "for their great act of courage." Tañada promised mass action and assured the minister and the general: "We won't stop until we get through the military barricade at Mendiola (the bridge leading to Malacañang)."

Former Congressman Jose "Peping" Cojuangco, Mrs. Aquino's elder brother, accompanied by Ambit Antonio and Tom Henson also called on Enrile and Ramos and promised they would use every means at their disposal to gather more people at the camp. Even Freddie Aguilar and Nora Aunor, a well-known pop singer and movie actress, were there to give Enrile and Ramos support. "The minister and the general united us all in a non-violent way," Aguilar said. Aunor later went around the camp and donated shirts and candies to the soldiers. "I believe in what they are doing," she said.

Before she left Cebu, Mrs. Aquino spoke to reporters and was evidently happy over the turn of events. She urged the nation to give its full support to Enrile and Ramos, and reiterated an appeal for Marcos to step down from office so that a peaceful transition of power could be made. She called the action of Ramos and Enrile a turning point in the peaceful struggle to unseat Marcos. The example of the two officials, she said, proved that there are government officials who are loyal to the Filipino people and the nation and not to individuals.

Mrs. Aquino disclosed she talked with Enrile late Saturday night. She asked Enrile the purpose of his action and he said he felt that Marcos did not have the mandate of the people and that she should rightfully assume the presidency. Mrs. Aquino then asked him to what extent he and Ramos would pursue their goals. The reply was, "Till the end."

★   ★   ★

Back in Camp Crame, Ramos told the press that Marcos' story about the aborted coup and assassination was a figment of Marcos' imagination. Enrile called it "a lot of bull."

"We are not interested in the assassination of Mr. Marcos," Ramos said. "We only want the improvement of our armed forces and our own government so they may better serve our people. We have no capability of inflicting violence. We are on a purely defensive stance here. However, we will not surrender and let the people down."

Ramos went down to join the people manning the human barricades and cheered them up. "You have no idea how it feels, this popular support," Ramos told a reporter.

"Finally, the military is once more the army of the people. For the first time in a long while, the people and the Army are working together," Ramos exulted. ☐

CHAPTER III

DAY 3

February 24, 1986

It is not a revolt, it is a revolution!

— Duc de Liancourt
in a letter to Louis XVI

It is to the interest of the commonwealth
of mankind that there should be someone
who is unconquered, someone against whom
fortune has no power.

— Seneca

THE TIDE TURNS

Embarrassed by the fiasco of the previous day, the Ver strategists at Fort Bonifacio spent the first hours of Day 3, February 24, 1986, looking for another way to "inject" Marines into Camp Aguinaldo, from where an assault on Camp Crame would be launched. Brawner was at the drawing board. At first, he thought of shuttling the Marines by air. Risky. The land route would be safer. Following a suggestion from Natividad, CDC units would be utilized to sweep away human barricades so that the Marines could enter Camp Aguinaldo by way of Libis and the Logistics Command Compound.

Balbas' 4th Marine Regiment was picked for the job and it was reinforced by armor: three LVTHs and three V-150s. Army CDC battalions would lead the way through EDSA turning right before Ortigas, going via Rodriguez street and then to Santolan by way of Libis, then push beyond the Logcom main gate.

Balbas' regiment and supporting units jumped off from Bonifacio at 4:14 a.m. This time the Marines moved more efficiently than they had on the previous day. The CDC units under the direction of Brig. Gen. Victor Natividad, using tear gas, breached the human barricades at Libis and by 6 a.m. were inside the Logcom compound. The Marines then poured into Camp Aguinaldo. Balbas got a briefing from Estrellado of ISAFP, not knowing that the unit had already joined the other side. Estrellado, tongue in cheek, gave an exaggerated picture of Camp Crame's strength.

★ ★ ★

The human barricades at the entrance to Camp Crame were stronger than those on the previous day because, as early as 5 a.m., Ramos had broadcast an appeal for more people. The crowd occupied the length and breadth of EDSA, from as far south as Ortigas and as far northwest as Cubao. Balbas' regiment, however, had avoided Ortigas and, besides, were on the road about an hour earlier.

Ramos reinforced his appeal by giving a bleak picture of the rebel defenses and a fearsome portrayal of the attacking force. "An overwhelming military force has been assembled and directed to move against us," Ramos said. He asked radio announcers: "Please tell the world it is Mr. Marcos who is now about to inflict violence, terror, and vengeance upon our people here in Camp Crame." Radio Veritas' June Keithley, whom General Ramos addressed on the air as "General Keithley," reported on the "deteriorating" defense situation to her listeners.

★ ★ ★

At Villamor Air Base to the south of Fort Bonifacio, Piccio, the Air Force commander, sensed cloud over the loyalty of his pilots and men. But he could not see how bad the problem was. Unknown to him, a Reformist group in the Air Force had been creeping into the base in the past several weeks to put in place secret plans for the paralyzation and capture of the base, if and when necessary.

It was not an afterthought that on the first day of the revolution, the telephone lines of the Air Force top brass were already being tapped and young officers with Reformist ideals kept a tight lip on what was going on.

Piccio leaned heavily on the 5th Strike Wing at the base for support to ground operations against Aguinaldo and Crame. The wing, combat-tested, had earned four streamers for its missions in Mindanao operations. At the time of the revolution, the wing was commanded by Col. Antonio E. Sotelo, like Enrile a Cagayanon. The wing had T-28 fighter bombers based at Sangley, where Sotelo had his headquarters. Its helicopters, most of them Sikorskys, were at Villamor.

Piccio did not know that Sotelo was with the other side. He had a 15th Strike Wing chopper take pictures of Crame and Aguinaldo on Day 2 of the revolution. This was allowed by Sotelo, who thought it to be harmless. Then two of his helicopters were used to provide air cover for the Marines on that same day. This was also all right with Sotelo, because he knew the gunships would not have to fire at anyone. But even then, he had plans to deliver his wing to Enrile; he was only waiting for the right time to move over to Camp Crame.

★   ★   ★

Day 1 of the revolution, Sotelo had pledged his support to Enrile. Here is how he explained his decision:

"At 52, I already had most of what I wanted in life: a wonderful family, a fruitful professional life. Now, there is this devastated country of ours, and two of the most decent among Filipinos begging help for their lives as they were being pursued by the most evil and sinister people I have known. So my mind was set to give my life, if need be, to my country and to the cause that these two gentlemen were fighting for."

Sotelo's predicament was that he did not know which of his pilots were thinking the same, and which were loyal to Marcos. Conversely, the pilots must have wondered which side their chief was on. Only Major Charles Hotchkiss, commander of the 20th Air Commando Squadron of the 15th Strike Wing, and Capt. Fernando Manalo of A-3, HPAF came to know that Sotelo had already committed himself to Enrile. And that was because when Hotchkiss and Manalo visited Sotelo at his quarters Saturday night, Manalo boldly told the Colonel: "Sir, we are laying down our cards on the table. I'm telling you that we are on the side of Minister Enrile and General Ramos." To which Sotelo retorted: "I'm with you."

On Day 2, word came from Ver to prepare two gunships for a mission to disable two helicopters at Crame. After briefing his pilots,

Sotelo asked, "Now, who of you gentlemen would like to volunteer for the mission?" Nobody moved. He asked each pilot the same question. No one volunteered. His conclusion: "I knew then that we were altogether." Fortunately the mission was scrapped by Marcos.

It was with a sense of joy and relief that Sotelo began to discuss with his pilots the plan to fight on the side of Enrile and Ramos. In the mid-afternoon of that Sunday, Sotelo took a small helicopter to Sangley to feel out the loyalty of the fighter-bomber commander who was his second in command. By a stroke of luck, just as Sotelo was trying to gauge where the officer's sentiments lay, the phone rang. A general was on the line, with the message that Marcos was the duly constituted authority and should be obeyed. This remark drew a comment from the officer: *"Ayon ang tama!"* ("That is correct!") It gave the officer away, and Sotelo devised a scheme to freeze the fighter-bombers.

★ ★ ★

Back at Villamor, at 3 a.m. on Monday, Day 3, Sotelo saw to it that the fighter-bombers would fly to Clark and stay there. At the base, the planes would be practically frozen by their empty tanks. The Americans were providing fuel only for the helicopters; they did not want any bombings to escalate the crisis.

At 4 a.m., Sotelo woke up the helicopter pilots. He briefed them at 5:15 a.m. Then he said, "Anybody who wants to back out, get out of this room and go home peacefully." Nobody stirred. Then he announced the plan to land at Crame at 6 a.m. He told the pilots: "Okay, guys, you die only once. It is a rare opportunity to die fighting for a cause."

★ ★ ★

Hotchkiss led the five Sikorsky gunships up into the sky at 5:55 a.m. They flew over Fort Bonifacio, made one pass over the Constabulary headquarters at Camp Crame, and Hotchkiss signalled they were coming in.

Crame was agog over the identity of the helicopters. Whose side were they on? Some soldiers cocked their guns instinctively. When Hotchkiss' dragonflies touched down at 6:10 a.m., the door opened and out jumped a crew member waving a white handkerchief. The crowd went into cheers and yells and ran towards the arrivals. Press photographers clicked their cameras, and TV and radio microphones were shoved at the pilots. Sotelo was mum. He said he had to see Enrile and Ramos first. A few minutes later, three more helicopters arrived: two Sikorsky rescue ships and a small utility BO-105.

At the command post, a misty-eyed Enrile gave Sotelo and everyone of his pilots a hug. If Malacañang could see them now, for just a few hours before the landing, Sotelo had orders from Piccio to take two gunships to Fort Bonifacio, and orders from Malacañang for the Sikorskys to attack Crame. Marcos and Ver had played into Sotelo's hands by giving him a cover for the flight to Crame, and now Crame was planning an intimidation attack on Malacañang.

Rebel operations chief Aguirre considered the defection of the air commando helicopters a turning point. Ramos nodded, "The tide has turned." Sotelo agreed wholeheartedly.

"News of the defection was a bombshell to General Ver," an aide of Ver recalled. "It furthered the confusion already prevailing in Malacañang."

★ ★ ★

At 6:27 a.m, Keithley was back on the air to announce: "Mr. Marcos, his wife, and son, Bongbong have just taken off from the Manila International Airport." Furthermore, "daughters Imee and Irene had left earlier," and Ver was left alone in the Palace. "You are not fighting for anything or anyone anymore," Keithley told the troops loyal to Marcos.

It was about this time that Balbas' boys were proceeding to occupy aggressive positions for the assault on Camp Crame. They had seen how the crowds along EDSA burst into a festive mood when Marcos' supposed departure was announced. Station DZRH also carried the report; the others waited for confirmation.

Marcos' rival for the presidency, Mrs. Aquino, broadcast a message of thanks to the people for supporting Enrile and Ramos, and asked the citizenry to continue peaceful and non-violent moves to protect the two leaders.

With jubilation in the air Enrile and Ramos came down from the Constabulary headquarters to join the merrymaking crowd, which had spilled into the camp grounds. Enrile was greeted with cheers of "Johnny, Johnny, Johnny."

He told the people: "Democracy has been restored to us. From this moment on, the armed forces are your armed forces, loyal to you, the people, the nation, and the Constitution, and not to any one man."

Keithley's report, it turned out, was a dud. It didn't seem to make a difference, however. The people were still in a triumphant mood, unmindful of the deployment of the assaulting force behind the walls of Camp Aguinaldo.

★ ★ ★

Ver's men were not taking anything for granted.

Balbas established his 4th Marine Provisional Brigade headquarters at the KKK Secretariat building at Camp Aguinaldo. The 3rd Marine Battalion occupied the golf course near the camp chapel. The 5th Marine Battalion occupied an area near the enlisted men's quarters and golf club building.

The Marines positioned eight 81 mm and 60 mm mortars and six recoil-less rifles at strategic places and zeroed in on their targets in Camp Crame. At the golf course fronting the camp were positioned three Landing Vehicle Tracked Howitzers. Three V-150 commando armored vehicles were positioned elsewhere.

Thus, in Camp Aguinaldo was the unusual situation of soldiers of opposing sides being in plain view of one another with nobody having the desire to shoot at the "enemy." Right within Aguinaldo were Lt. Col. Jerry Albano and his Security and Escort Battalion of 200 officers and men, a unit of GHQ command that decided on the first day of the revolution to join the troops protecting Enrile and Ramos. Albano, on this Monday, was wearing the miniature Philippine flag as shoulder patch which Enrile and Ramos and everybody else in the rebel camp was wearing. On this day, the flag had the sun pointed down to indicate it was Day 3 of the revolution. The patch was turned clockwise 90 degrees every day, starting with the sun up.

Also in the camp were soldiers belonging to the "El Diablo" group dedicated to reform at the enlisted men's level and to deal with organized crime with a mailed fist. This group was disbanded on orders of Marcos but they emerged as a fighting unit when they came to know of the revolution. They took positions observing the left flank of Balbas' troops. Albano's battalion poised to hit from the right. At Balbas' rear, some distance away to be out of sight, was Task Force Delta composed of Camp Crame constables. Although these rebel units had Balbas' Marines boxed in, they would not be taking any hostile action. Their orders were not to fire unless fired upon.

★ ★ ★

At 9 a.m., Balbas heard through his hand-held radio this order from Ramas: "Fire your howitzers at objective (Crame) and report compliance immediately." The automatic reply was, "Yes, Sir." But Balbas did not transmit the command.

At 9:10 a.m., Ramas again told Balbas: "I say again, fire your howitzers at objective and report compliance immediately. President Marcos is on the other line waiting for the result." Balbas replied, "Yes, Sir. I am now positioning my howitzers." Immediately, Balbas tried to

contact Tadiar to check if Ramas' order had really been cleared by
Marcos. Balbas was told Tadiar had gone to Malacañang. He tried to
reach Brawner but nobody knew where Brawner was.

At 9:20 a.m., Ramas again barked the command through the radio: "Colonel, fire your howitzers now." The reply: "Sir, I am still
positioning the cannons."

After frantic efforts with the telephone, Balbas finally got connected with Tadiar, who was at the Community Hall in Malacañang
Park with other generals. Malacañang had again summoned the generals to be on television with Marcos that morning to disprove Keithley's
report that the President and his family had left the country.

Balbas informed Tadiar excitedly over the telephone: "Sir, I have
been receiving orders from General Ramas to fire the LVTH6s at
Camp Crame. Is this cleared by Malacañang?"

"All right, wait for a while and I will verify," was Tadiar's reply.
Ver assured him the order had been cleared by Marcos.

Tadiar returned to the telephone and told Balbas: "The order to
fire is confirmed. You can fire."

Balbas complained, "Sir, I just cannot fire. We will be killing
thousands of civilians."

"I understand that," Tadiar said. "You can use your discretion."

★ ★ ★

On the other side, meanwhile, Hotchkiss' squadron got its first mission: cripple the Malacañang radio transmitter. One Sikorsky gunship
was sent up. It returned within minutes. The pilot could not see the
transmitter.

A second mission was immediately given to the same pilots, Capt.
Wilfredo Evangelista and his co-pilot, 1st Lt. Richelieu Halago, whose

job would make them a William Tell if they could inflict "just the desired amount of damage." They were to hit the apple and not the boy on whose head it rested. They were to hit Malacañang with a few rockets to rattle, but not hurt, its occupants. In Enrile's view, the attack would have the psychological effect of impressing upon the minds of Marcos and his generals that the rebels had the edge in air capability and could hit any target at will.

★ ★ ★

In Malacañang, Marcos had another sleepless night. Flabbergasted by Keithley's report of his departure, he ordered Cendaña his information minister, to put him and his family on television to disprove the story. Cendaña was to encourage reporters to ask Marcos questions on up-to-the-minute developments to show that it was a live, not pre-taped telecast.

Outside the Palace, the crowds were pounding at the gates, demanding that the guards let them in because the Marcoses had left.

Among the reporters who came early in response to Cendaña's invitation to the press conference was Vic Tañedo, who saw Mrs. Marcos crying in the President's study. Marcos was talking into the telephone, and Tañedo guessed it was President Reagan at the other end because Marcos was saying, "But, Mr. President, I have to do this."

When Mrs. Marcos stepped out of the study, her eyes now dry, she was met by reporter Amy Pamintuan, who told her about the mob outside. Mrs. Marcos said she would take her car and ride out there where she would wave at the people to prove that the Marcoses were still in the country. Mrs. Marcos had gone down to board her car when Marcos emerged from his study and had aides call her back. Marcos told her to wake up the children for their TV appearance.

★ ★ ★

The press conference, televised over Channel 4, began at 9:30 a.m. at the Reception Hall. Surrounding Marcos were his wife, daughter Irene and husband Greggy Araneta, and Marcos' grandchildren. Later, they were joined by Imee and husband Tommy Manotoc, and Gov. Ferdinand Marcos II, still in fatigue uniform, and Aimee, a ward of the Marcoses. Cendaña and Imelda's cousin, Babes Romualdez, supervised the proceedings.

Besides the Marcos clan, there were Ver and sons Irwin and Rexor, Ochoco and a few generals.

Marcos announced he was declaring a state of emergency. He ordered all radio stations to stop the broadcasts of troop movements and the statements of Enrile and Ramos which he said were causing panic among the people. He said he had authorized his troops to seize all stations that did not comply. The troops were also to defend all vital installations but only with small arms.

"I am taking my oath tomorrow, and I intend to stay as President," Marcos stressed.

While Marcos was answering questions from the press, Ver edged closer to the President, obviously eager to have a word with him.

"Sir, we cannot keep retreating all the time. They are massing civilians against our troops. They are engaged in a massive disinformation campaign. We are still in control of the situation. We came here to show you that we are strong, we are organized, and we are ready to neutralize them. We are ready to annihilate them, to destroy them. Just give me the order, Sir, and we will hit them."

Ver was trembling in anger. He talked about Air Force planes that had taken off, and were ready to mount an attack on Camp Crame.

These were the two fighter-bombers seen after Sotelo's helicopters had landed in the camp, as if to follow up the gunship attack that never was. The planes circled over Crame, tilted their wings and flew off in the direction of Clark. Their pilots had orders to bomb the camp, but they didn't carry out their orders. The pilots were rebel officers.

Marcos tried to calm down Ver. But he did not tell Ver to forget the annihilation idea. In truth, Balbas, whose howitzers were trained at Crame, already had confirmation from Ver through Tadiar that Marcos had cleared Ramas' order for the cannon lanyards to be pulled. It was Balbas' authority from Tadiar to use his discretion that kept the guns silent.

★ ★ ★

At 9:56 a.m., the TV monitor in Malacañang's Reception Hall went blank. Cendaña fiddled with the knobs and saw that the other channels were on the air. Col. Arturo Aruiza, one of the President's aides, said that the rebels had taken Channel 4.

With the fall of Channel 4 into rebel hands, Marcos hardened his position. He said he was lifting his policy of maximum tolerance toward the rebels in Camp Crame. Of the human barricades, he said, "If you are going to be frightened by 2,000 civilians (around Crame) then let's not talk about running a government." Marcos evidently was getting the wrong figures because there were already more than a million people around the camps, and another million massed in other parts of the city in accordance with Ramos' strategy of blockading the North Diversion road, massing around television and radio stations and creating diversionary demonstrations at Mendiola and Nagtahan streets near the Palace. The crowds continued to swell by the hour.

★ ★ ★

As the press conference was going on, about 4,000 followers of Mrs. Aquino demonstrating along Mendiola street were dispersed with warning shots and water cannons by presidential security troops. During the melee, people in the crowd carried away a number of barbed wire accordions placed across Mendiola and then cut the wire for distribution as souvenirs. This was to distract the Palace defenders away from the oncoming helicopter attack.

★ ★ ★

Reporters leaving the Palace after the press conference saw soldiers on the top floor of the Administration building pointing excitedly at something in the sky. Soldiers manning the tanks were alerted and those at Gate 4 talked into their handy-talkies as their eyes scanned the sky. The reporters ran back to the Malacañang newsroom to take cover.

★ ★ ★

Capt. Wildredo Evangelista was up in his Sikorsky gunship with the mission of a "counter-intimidation" attack on Malacañang. He went out to Manila Bay and then circled back. He hid himself among the buildings at Rizal Park, then popped up behind the Manila Post Office, and in seconds was poised to fire at the Palace. He fired six rockets. They exploded in various places — near the First Lady's bedroom, at the Palace garden and in the parking area. Three cars were damaged, one of them Greggy Araneta's Mercedez Benz. Two helicopters were damaged. A constabulary officer, three enlisted men, and two civilians suffered minor injuries. An officer in Malacañang said, "We're lucky the injuries were slight. But the psychological damage was great."

The attack came so fast that although many handheld guns blazed at the helicopter as it sped over the Palace, only one bullet, probably from an Armalite, went through its right side. Anti-aircraft guns in the tanks failed to fire. Soldiers picked up rocket fragments on the Malacañang grounds. These were identified to be from 75mm anti-personal rockets.

Inside the Palace, the generals and other officers scrambled for armored vests. The First Family was huddled in a room and came out of the attack unscathed. The troops appeared discouraged. Marcos went through the incident calmly. Then he was angry. Cendaña knew that another press conference was in the offing.

★ ★ ★

The rocket attack on Malacañang sent Ochoco calling for a conference at 3 p.m. to plan the defense of Malacañang and counteraction to regain ground lost to Enrile and Ramos. The outcome of the meeting was the organization of a Malacañang Defense Group with Ochoco as chief; Brawner as his assistant for operations. The group intended to retake television and radio stations already in rebels hands.

★ ★ ★

Back at Camp Aguinaldo, another order came from Ramas to fire the howitzers and mortars at Crame. Balbas came back with a familiar tune, "Sir, we are looking for maps and positioning the cannons and mortars."

Shortly after Malacañang was hit by rockets, Col. Irwin Ver gave the order to Balbas to fire cannons and mortars and assault Crame. Ver said Malacañang was under air attack, and there were 10 casualties. This was followed by a call from Tadiar asking if Balbas had fired as ordered. Balbas came out with the same tune: "Sir, there is danger that there would be an unacceptable number of civilian casualties."

Then Ramas told Balbas: "General Oropesa is going there by helicopter to supervise the operation." Balbas received more orders from Ramas to fire the cannons and mortars until he was fed up. He simply disregarded Ramas.

★ ★ ★

★ ★ ★

Gador of the "Cagayan 100" intercepted the message about Oropesa's going to Camp Aguinaldo. It was time to destroy all the helicopters at the Villamor Air Base and deny Oropesa the means to get to Aguinaldo.

★ ★ ★

Balbanero, the peacekeeper at Camp Aguinaldo, was worried about the presence of contending forces a nose away from where he stood. Just one shot, and the whole place would be converted into a bloody cauldron, he knew. A single order from Oropesa to Balbas' boys to fire and it would be the beginning of a civil war.

At noon, Balbanero rang up Albano, although he knew the latter was already on the other side. He told Albano, "Hurry up and go to Colonel Balbas and persuade him to desist from carrying out his order to shell Crame." Albano sought Balbas on the double. Albano saw the artillery and mortar crew set to fire. As he approached Balbas, Marines surrounded the visitor with a rebel patch. Balbas, sweating in the noonday sun, his face creased with deep lines, growled at the rebel officer. "What do you want?" he asked.

"I was instructed to see you, Sir," Albano replied.

"What for?"

"To request, please, that you will not proceed with your plan to fire at Camp Crame. Can we talk this over, Sir? You know fully well there are many civilians out there who are going to be killed if you fire."

"But I have my instructions," Balbas countered.

"Yes, Sir, you have your instructions." Albano declared. "But I also have mine, that is, the moment you fire, my troops will assault you and fight it out with you. I pray we will not have to come to that point. After all, we are all comrades."

Balbas was silent. Albano, intending to buy time, said, "Sir, General Balbanero would like to talk with you about the matter."

"Okay, tell General Balbanero to come here," Balbas conceded.

Albano was taken aback. This was the first time a colonel was asking a general to see him. But Albano felt he was getting the time he wanted.

Smiling, he told Balbas, "All right, Sir, I'll get General Balbanero to talk to you. Please, hold off any action until the two of you can talk."

On the way to Balbanero, Albano called up Col. Honasan at Camp Crame to inform him of Balbas' position. Honasan answered, "Okay, Mistah, get General Balbanero to talk to Colonel Balbas. But in the event the talks bog down, you can be sure that with the fall of the first mortar round here, our Sikorskys will take off and take care of the Marines. Be then prepared to follow through and assault him."

★ ★ ★

Balbanero went to see Balbas, but by that time, the latter had already received instructions from Tadiar. This was the conversation:

Tadiar: For your info, Malacañang has been strafed by helicopter. Have you already fired?

Balbas: With the developments now, it is impossible, Sir. I am already surrounded by hostile forces. If I make any aggressive move, my unit will suffer heavy casualties.

Tadiar: Can you extricate yourself from your position?

Balbas: It's hard, Sir.

Tadiar: Now, here's what you will do. Establish a modus vivendi
with the hostile forces. Tell them you are withdrawing.
Then take your unit back to Bonifacio right away.

Balbas: Yes, Sir.

Balbas' unit pulled out of Camp Aguinaldo by way of the Logistics Command. By 12:30 p.m. the Marines were taking the route along
Rodriguez avenue and Shaw boulevard to home. The human barricades along Shaw broke ranks for the Marines to go through
smoothly.

Upon reporting to Tadiar, Balbas found he had been relieved of
his command of the 4th Marine Provisional Brigade. He was to return
to his regular assignment as commanding officer of the Combat Service Support Brigade. He had the queer feeling that he had been hastily
pulled out of Camp Aguinaldo because he was under suspicion. Did
his comrades think he would be marching with his troops to Crame to
join Ramos? He had heard rumors that he would be arrested for repeated disobedience to Ramas' orders. But he was prepared to face the
music: "I could only say that any order to kill innocent civilians is
unlawful and must not be obeyed. I only followed the dictates of my
conscience."

★   ★   ★

At noon, when the tension at Camp Crame eased with the withdrawal of the Marines from Camp Aguinaldo, the rebel helicopters
were told to make a pre-emptive strike at Villamor Air Base. Sotelo
told Hotchkiss to do it with three Sikorskys. On the way to the base,
Hotchkiss got these orders from Sotelo: "Look for helicopters, Huey
or whatever, anywhere in the air or on the ground and shoot them."

The three helicopters flew over Bonifacio. There was no helicopter on the ground there. They then turned to Villamor. There were five

helicopters aligned at the flight line with crew obviously preparing the aircraft.

Hotchkiss caught their radio frequency and said: "I ask you to vacate the area. Get out of the helicopters and just vanish because I have orders to fire. Repeat, I have orders to destroy the helicopters."

The reply came a voice of utter helplessness: "Come and get it."

Hotchkiss' office was close to the target area. He remembered that one of his people, the only one left behind, would still be there. He radioed the office: "Get out of the office quickly and run to the flight line and tell all the people there to vacate the place."

Capt. Ramon Cruz at Camp Crame was apprehensive. He radioed Hotchkiss: "Charles, see to it they all move away. *Mga bata ko iyan:* (Those are my people.)"

When the tarmac was cleared, the raiders strafed the five helicopters on the ground with 50 caliber bullets. All were completely crippled. One exploded. No other aircraft was hit. There were also C-130s, Fokkers, Nomads and other planes there. Not one of them grazed by a single bullet. It was a neat job.

★ ★ ★

At 1 p.m. Ver gave secret orders to Piccio to launch an air attack on Crame. Piccio replied, "But Sir, we have no more gunships. They have just been destroyed."

Ver looked around for pilots at Malacañang. He got a few. But he could not give them planes. The fighter-bombers were at Clark without gas.

Desperate, Ver decided on letting Ramas do something. It took him an hour before he was connected to Ramas at Fort Bonifacio. Ver described how Crame could be attacked with the use of Army and Marine troops who were still loyal. Ramas was cool to the idea. Ver insisted. Ramas just refused to go along.

Ramas was getting tired with the series of unsuccessful attempts to hit a sitting duck like Camp Crame. Although the operations looked very simple on paper, he was flattered that in the crunch, Ver had looked to him for help. It hurt him to see things being bungled above and below him. There were instances when orders which should have gone down the chain of command bypassed his post. There were indications that Marcos himself was losing his faith in Ver's ability to protect the First Family, one being his establishment of direct communications with Ramas. Even Ver's operations center at Malacañang Park was the laughing stock of officers who called it a center of confusion.

As Brawner was to size up the operations center: "General Ver never knew how to utilize his staff fully. The operations center at the Park was in reality a monitoring center. J2 (Intelligence) and J3 (Operations) had nobody to assist them as their personnel were left behind at Camp Aguinaldo. The action was at Camp Aguinaldo. The commander and staff were far from the critical point."

As for the confusion, this portion of Brawner's analysis sheds light on the tragi-comic affair: "There is something wrong in the AFP's structure and the systems developed which allows indecisiveness among unit commanders. Authority is inadequate when commanders have to personally hear from higher commanders (the brass at the Park) before taking action. This results in the loss of precious time. Moreover, when commanders become glued to the phone and have no time to attend to important problems and make relevant decisions, they forget to make an estimate of their situation."

Even funnier, the operations center was used to take care of Ver's personal problems. At 3 p.m. Ver directed Col. Romeo Ochoco of the Air Force who was at the center, to arrange for the evacuation of his close friend, Mrs. Edna Camcam and her children.

★ ★ ★

Tadiar was alerted at 4:30 p.m. to prepare one Marine battalion to operate with Army elements in an assault on Crame. But evidently tired of doing the same thing over and over again, he immediately went to his headquarters, summoned all his staff officers and unit commanders, and called for a consensus. The consensus: the Marines would no longer take part in military operations that would result in the unnecessary death or wounding of innocent civilians. There were no objections to defensive operations for the protection of the President.

Tadiar then went to the Army conference room for discussions on the new plan to attack Crame as ordered by Marcos. The plan was to use elements of the 42nd Infantry Battalion from Quezon province and elements of the Marines for the assault on Crame. The route to be taken from Bonifacio to the objective was Nagtahan, Greenhills, and Santolan. A reconnaisance team was sent out to try the route. It came back with the report that hundreds of thousands of people were barricading the way. Civilian casualties could not be avoided. Ramas and Oropesa asked Abadia for his recommendation. Abadia was for informing Marcos that the plan was not feasible. Marcos agreed, but asked that other options be explored.

The next plan was for a mortar attack on Crame from Rosario bridge in Pasig about 3.4 kilometers away. Abadia said "no." Palafox recommended that the 54th Infantry Battalion move from Camp Aquino to Fort Bonifacio for the attack. Abadia and Ramas vetoed the idea. No new plan was sent up to Marcos.

"At this time, options were really dwindling."

Abadia sent his emissary, Col. Abraham Paray, secretly to Camp Crame to get in touch with classmates and other PMA alumni, especially with Col. Ismael Villareal at Crame operations, to convey the sentiments of PMA people in Fort Bonifacio that they should take all possible measures to avoid bloodshed. The message was well taken at Camp Crame.

★ ★ ★

The will to fight was waning most perceptibly among the Rangers, who had been beefed up to regimental strength by Ver not only for their counterinsurgency capability but also because they could be a resource for the defense of Malacañang. Ver saw in Brawner a dependable officer. But on Day 3 of the Revolution, Ver was beginning to hear reports that the Rangers were "becoming unreliable."

As if to confirm Ver's worst doubts, even Mrs. Brawner was exerting her own pressure on her husband to join the other side. She called him up to report that Commodore Tagumpay Jardiniano and some other PMA classmates were already in Camp Crame. Brawner told her he could not leave the operations center in Malacañang. The pressure kept up from unwitting sources. In the afternoon, after the rocket attack on Malacañang, Col. Romeo Lim phoned Brawner from Ranger headquarters to report a "serious morale problem" among the troops. Brawner asked Ver for permission to go to his headquarters. Ver declined. Brawner called up Ramas, and Ramas said he would consult Marcos. After ten minutes, Ver told Brawner he may go, but he should convince his boys to do their duty.

At Fort Bonifacio, Brig. Gen. Ramon Cannu told Brawner to talk to his men at once because they were unwilling to go on a mission directed by Marcos. Brawner summoned all the Ranger officers and told them he had made up his mind not to comply with that mission order, either. He warned them that this decision should not be known to adjacent units because they could move against the Rangers. He asked the officers to explain the situation to their men.

Brawner then informed Cannu that the Rangers were not carrying out the mission. Cannu pleaded for reconsideration.

"That is final," Brawner declared, and relayed his decision to Camp Crame. Later that night, Brawner learned that the mortars of an adjacent unit were trained on Marine headquarters. Crame's reaction was a plan to send Col. Servando Bucao during the night to spirit Brawner out of Bonifacio. But Brawner said he would stick it out with his boys.

★　★　★

While military activity seemed to be ebbing, the human barricades maintained their ground. They would leave only upon orders of the rebel command.

Policemen in the municipality of Makati organized themselves to beef up the barricades. Fort Bonifacio is within the territorial jurisdiction of that town through which EDSA the main approach to Camp Crame runs. Along EDSA is strategic Guadalupe bridge which, if closed, could bottle up Fort Bonifacio. The policemen, in a civic group known as the Eagles of Makati, got the drivers of buses, garbage trucks, jeepneys and cars to park across the approach to Guadalupe bridge to block tanks and troops. It was an effective metal barricade that firmed up the human barricades along EDSA.

It was in that barricade where Brig. Gen. Ramon Montaño, AFP Anti-Narcotics Command chief, was stopped in his car while on his way to join Enrile and Ramos in Camp Crame. Mistaken as a loyalist, Montaño, after properly identifying himself, had to get off his car and walked eight kilometers on EDSA to get to the camp. "The crowd was so thick it was impossible to get to the camp by car," he recalled later.

A convoy of troops reached that point in the afternoon, then decided to turn back into the Fort. Until the end of the revolution, the Eagles of Makati, were given missions by Camp Crame. They were led by Policeman First Class Ernesto Sales.

★ ★ ★

Day 3 was also marked by skirmishes for possession of television and radio stations, so vital to both sides for generating popular support. It was Ver's error that at the very start of the revolution he did not secure the government's hold on these communications links. Instead, he wasted his time scheming with his crony generals at an operations center that was not working as it should. An aide of Ver said "the morale began to sag" among the defenders of Malacañang when they learned of the fall of Channel 4 to the rebels.

The rebels were prepared for the battle to control the airlanes. It was for this purpose that Task Force Delta was organized as soon as Enrile and Ramos announced the withdrawal of their support from Marcos. Delta was composed of elements of the Constabulary Security Group commanded by Lt. Col. Eduardo S. Matillano; a contingent of the Constabulary Highway Patrol Group led by Lt. Col. Francisco Zubia, Jr.; and a Narcotics Command contingent under Lt. Col. Teodorico Viduya.

It was Delta that captured the Maharlika Broadcasting System Channel 4 complex on Bohol avenue, Quezon City, about 4 kilometers north of Camp Crame. The building and installations in the compound were defended by 12 Rangers, a couple of security guards and the chief security officer, Army Lt. Col. Benito Runas. There were about 40 employees inside.

The Delta team surrounded the place and demanded the surrender of the occupants. Besides Channel 4, the compound housed the National Media Production Center, Philippine News Agency, Bureau of Broadcast, Voice of the Philippines radio network, and other government broadcast stations. There were negotiations for surrender, with the assistance of Col. Mariano Santiago. The talks failed, a firefight ensued. One Ranger was wounded and five surrendered. Six were captured in mopping-up operations. The employees were detained for a while and then released. One of them, a technician, was injured. Another, named Fred Arias, had a heart attack and died.

With Channel 4 in their hands, the Delta troopers organized the security of the premises. There were human barricades in the streets outside, many of them manned by members of AKMA, Bayan, and ATOM, the group of Butz Aquino. Troops in two 6 × 6 trucks sent by Ver to retake Channel 4 sized up Delta team and the human barricades, then took a U-turn homeward. Some of Ver's troops tried to regroup at Scout Albano and Panay streets but withdrew after a firefight. One of them, a draftee, was wounded.

★ ★ ★

At 1:30 p.m. Channel 4 was on the air in the service of the rebel cause. At 2 p.m. troop reinforcements with V-150 armored vehicles arrived from Camp Crame to augment the Delta team.

But Malacañang had not yet given up the idea of retaking Channel 4. A plan was drawn to have it recaptured by Rangers and armored units. But experience having proved the Rangers to be "unreliable," they were erased from the plan. Only armor was to be utilized. At sundown, an armored column rolled out of Fort Bonifacio and took the Nagtahan route. When it reached Sta. Mesa, it was halted by human barricades.

"What do you recommend?" Ramas asked Abadia. The answer: "Tell the President to recall the column." Marcos did so. There were no further plans to repossess Channel 4.

However, the Delta team continued to protect the government compound through strict security measures. Other Delta elements were elsewhere to keep an eye on Radio Veritas and other broadcasting installations as well as to help the defenders of Camp Aguinaldo. In the afternoon, a demolition team of Task Force Delta blew up portions of the highway in Binangonan and Teresa in Rizal province to block troops of the 2nd Infantry Division from moving into Manila.

As for the intelligence work necessary for the security of Channel 4, the Delta team noted that Colonel Santiago was helpful in organizing civilian volunteers for information gathering. Ham Radio Philippines was also helpful in monitoring the movements of Marcos forces. Ham information was "efficient and effective."

The next worry of Task Force Delta was Channel 9 where Ver had kept a bunch of snipers. But the Deltans were confident of meeting the new challenge because of their successes at Channel 4 and Radio Veritas.

In Bulacan province to the north, the Constabulary secured the transmitter of Station DZRH at Malanday and another facility at Karuhatan in Valenzuela town. Here the Constabulary rallied the people to set up barricades. Strategic portions of the highways in Malolos, Baliuag, and Meycauayan were also blocked by people power.

With the use of Channel 4 definitely denied Marcos, arrangements were made for a televised interview with the President on Channel 9. Retired Brig. Gen. Pacifico Lopez de Leon was sent out for this chore but Cendaña did not invite any reporter to cover the event. An aide of Cendaña explained: "The President does not want to talk with the Press Corps anymore. He does not want them to see how empty the Palace is."

★ ★ ★

The Administration building was practically deserted. Employees had started leaving since the early afternoon. They feared another helicopter attack. The soldiers looked sullen, dismayed with news of continuing defections. There was talk among some officers of blowing up Channel 4, and someone said the station could be put out of commission by merely destroying the top 15 feet of its tower. The next question was how. With a fighter plane? a helicopter? a recoilless gun? Suddenly the idea was banished. Channel 4 was now working beautifully for Enrile and Ramos, augmented by Radio Veritas, DZRH, DZXL, DZFE, DZAS, DZMB, and independent provincial radio stations.

★ ★ ★

At 6 p.m. Marcos was on Channel 9 being interviewed by a panel composed of Pacifico Lopez de Leon, Ruther Batuigas, and Frankie Evangelista. The panel was in the studio, Marcos was in Malacañang. Only the panel could be seen on television because the link to Malacañang had been removed with the "demise" of Channel 4.

Marcos complained bitterly about the helicopter attack. "My family is cowering in terror inside Malacañang Palace because of this threat of bombing by helicopters . . . We even suspect that they might hit us with mortars." He pleaded with Enrile and Ramos: Stop this illegal activity." He added, "They have no moral, legal, or political basis for asking power from the people."

"They were the aggressors all along," Marcos emphasized. "Now, there is a reason for us to react with all the power and strength at our disposal." He promised, "There will be action within the next few days."

On reports of skirmishes and casualties, Marcos said, *"Sila ang nagsimula."* (They started it.) Then he warned of an escalation of the conflict: *"Nanganganib ang Republika ng Pilipinas. Hindi ko gusto, dahil pag nasimulan, tuloy-tuloy na 'yan. Ngunit pinipigilan din namin baka mayroon pang pag-uusapan."* (The Republic of the Philippines is in peril. I do not like this because once it starts, it's going to continue all the way. But I am restraining myself because there could still be a chance to talk things over.)

He was willing to talk with Enrile and Ramos, he said, "no matter what wounds they have inflicted on me."

Marcos repeated his opinion that Enrile was creating a "third force" bent on taking power from Mrs. Aquino. Told about the plan of a rump session of the Batasang Pambansa (parliament) to proclaim the election of Mrs. Aquino, Marcos commented, "The whole thing is completely illegal and unconstitutional."

Asked by Batuigas if he would impose curfew, Marcos replied, "Now that you've mentioned it, I am hereby declaring that curfew be observed from 6 p.m. to 6 a.m." It was 6:30 p.m. as he talked, but the millions on the streets laughed it off. There were not enough jails to hold them.

★ ★ ★

At Camp Crame, Enrile ridiculed the idea: "How can Mr. Marcos say he has the capacity to govern when he cannot even enforce his publicly announced curfew order?"

★ ★ ★

Despite the curfew, Marcos encouraged his followers to come to Malacañang that night and demonstrate their own brand of people power. Gate 4 would be open for them and they could stay on the grounds until the following day, when he would take his oath of office. He said they would be issued small arms to defend themselves against counter-demonstrators.

I'm sure there will be bloody clashes; if that's what Enrile and Ramos want, we'll do it," he said. "That's why I am calling on all loyalists to assemble at Malacañang."

In response, hundreds went to Malacañang on foot and in vehicles from the city and the neighboring provinces as far as Batangas. By midnight, there were about 2,000 barricading J. P. Laurel street up to the Ayala bridge.

Marcos declared: "We are here, we are not going to abandon the presidency. We have no intention of resigning. We have no intention of going abroad. We are here, and we will defend the Republic to our last breath, to the last drop of our blood."

But at the news desk of one of the dailies, an editor shared the information he had picked up that the Marcoses would soon leave Malacañang with American assistance.

★ ★ ★

At Camp Crame, Enrile revealed to reporters that Marcos had orders during the day for the camp to be bombed and strafed, but nobody obeyed them. It could only mean that the forces on the other side had lost their will to fight.

"Marcos has realized that we already had the capacity to inflict damage on him, so that he was restrained to that extent," Enrile said.

★ ★ ★

Throughout the day an uneasy Ver continued pawn-pushing his military units. He ordered Regional Unified Command No. 4 to send reinforcements to Malacañang, and got a battalion-size force composed of elements from the Cavite, Laguna, and Quezon Constabulary and regional headquarters.

Ver asked for more Marines from Bataan, but was told they could not leave the province without sacrificing the security of vital installations, so Palafox dispatched to Malacañang a company from the 5th Infantry Division.

Ver asked Brig. Gen. Jose Ma. Zumel to alert the 5th Fighter Wing for a mission. Zumel advised against this because many pilots were already on the side of the rebels.

★ ★ ★

In Camp Crame, Ramos updated his announcements of defections from the Marcos camp. The 5th Fighter Wing had switched its loyalty to Enrile. The two fighters Marcos sent to bomb Crame but headed straight for the Clark freezer instead, were from this wing.

True to Mrs. Brawner's information, Commodore Tagumpay Jardiniano, chief of the Naval Defense Force, was already in Crame. Brig. Gen. Augustus Paiso, chief of plans and programs; Col. Luis Ridao and Lt. Cdr. Ben Ocampo of the Judge Advocate General's Office; Brig. Gen. Cesar Tapia, head of Regional Unified Command No. 12;

and Col. Godofredo Rios, director of the Armed Forces Medical Center, had all reported to Crame.

Regional Unified Commands Nos. 2, 4, 5, 6, 8, 9, and 12 and all Constabulary and Integrated National Police regional commands, as well as the Constabulary Metropolitan Command had come over to the rebel side. As had the Clark Air Base Command under Col. Romeo David, Strategic Intelligence Training School, Naval Reserve Command, Army intelligence and engineering units, and Military Intelligence Group. The remaining troops of RUC-4, Ver's milking cow, flatly told their commander, Brig. Gen. Andres Ramos, that they were already with the Crame side.

The defecting naval forces led by Capt. Carlito Cunanan carried along their units, so the warships at Manila Bay had their guns pointed at Malacañang. Air power was almost completely in rebels hands with the defection of air bases in the Visayas and Mindanao. Brig. Gen. Ramon Farolan, who was with Enrile from Day 1, assumed command of the Air Force. He broadcast a warning that all armored units in the north coming down to the aid of Malacañang would be destroyed by gunships. No one moved.

Ramos also announced the defection of the Aviation Security Command (Avsecom). The security of the Manila International Airport was bolstered by troops flown in from the Bicol region. The rebels could now monitor departures from the country. They considered the possibility of Marcos, or at least some of his diehard supporters, leaving by air. Airline companies had suspended flights to foreign countries by Day 3.

★ ★ ★

By the end of Day 3, Enrile and Ramos had effective control over about 90 percent of the 250,000-man Armed Forces. Malacañang was left with its internal security force with 5,000 supporting troops.

Isolated, 20 kilometers to the east, was the 2nd Infantry Division of Brig. Gen. Ronald Pattugalan. Crame and Aguinaldo and its fringes were supported by more than 7,000 defecting soldiers.

★ ★ ★

Ramos declared the birth of the New Armed Forces of the Philippines (NAFP), to be run according to the best traditions and standards of the military profession.

Ramos stressed the military had no intention of using force to destroy Malacañang or compel Marcos to capitulate. He said, "We are hoping that he will voluntarily step down." The defenders would launch an offensive only if Ver's forces provoked that action, Ramos explained.

"We are keeping the lines of communication with Malacañang open," Enrile said. "We are willing to give Mr. Marcos and family safe passage out of the country."

With the control of the armed forces having shifted to Camp Crame, the turning point had been reached where the end of the Marcos regime was in sight. Retired Brig. Gen. Mario Espina, who was with Enrile since the start of the revolution, had predicted on the afternoon of Day 1 that Marcos' forces would capitulate in less than 72 hours.

★ ★ ★

Enrile met with Ernesto Maceda and other representatives of Mrs. Aquino. He thought it was imperative that a civilian government be set up to supplant the Marcos regime and provide stability for the country as it worked its way forward to a newfound horizon that was coming into view. He suggested Camp Crame as venue for the inaugural ceremonies for Mrs. Aquino and Senator Laurel. But the preference of the Aquino envoys was Club Filipino in San Juan, Metro Manila, which as history goes was the birthplace of the women's rights movement during the days of Spanish rule.

Marcos, on the other hand, changed his mind about his inauguration at the Quirino grandstand on Rizal Park. He would be sworn in at the Ceremonial Hall in Malacañang at high noon on the 25th of February as ordained by law. The diplomatic corps was not invited.

★ ★ ★

The United States government showed keen interest in verifying Enrile's claim that almost the entire armed forces were now with him and General Ramos. Washington evidently did not want to fall into the trap of abandoning Marcos when he still had the military. Earlier, Ambassador Philip Habib, President Reagan's personal representative, had assessed the situation. He had talked with both Marcos and Mrs. Aquino, and had also visited Enrile, Sin, and other personalities who provided him with the information Washington needed.

Also in town was Navy Capt. Carlos Agustin, defense attache at the Philippine Embassy in Washington, D.C., who set up an Intelligence Task Force for the Reformists. On Day 3, American military authorities at the United States embassy in Manila and agents of the State Department sought Agustin's help in piecing together an accurate report for Washington on the military aspect of the situation in Manila. They asked Agustin for data on the military forces that had defected to Enrile and Ramos, as against those still loyal to Marcos, as of 9 p.m., February 24.

They would rush the report to Washington. This, they said, would figure in the American government's efforts to persuade Marcos to leave the Philippines.

Agustin met his deadline. His input showed the rebels definitely had the upper hand.

It was evident, however, that even before nightfall on Day 3 of the revolution, Washington had decided to exert pressure on Marcos to abandon the presidency and leave the country, to avoid bloodshed.

The worm turned as dawn broke upon the millions on EDSA. □

CHAPTER IV

DAY 4

February 25, 1986

A good general not only sees the way to victory: he also knows when victory is impossible.

— Polybus

THE FLIGHT OF THE MAHARLIKA

As the revolution moved into its fourth day, the defenders of Malacañang remained on alert. But they were now more concerned with speculations on their Old Man's next move than with any possible attack on the Palace. The fact was that they had more men than was necessary for its defense.

As the defenders waited for dawn, these thoughts went through the mind of a young lieutenant: "The situation is a sad one for President Marcos. It is a choice between resigning or setting up a government in exile." A brother officer made a bet Marcos would never resign. In fact Marcos was determined to take his oath at noon, and there was no announcement about any change of plans.

Captain Fernando Golez, General Ver's aide-de-camp, wrote in his notebook: "I could see and feel the signs — they were ominous. I knew they were clearly seen and felt by the Palace troops, too. Quite admirably, they held on to their ground in spite of the overpowering odds against them. They seemed to be prepared for any eventuality. I presumed we acted this way because of a duty we had to perform, not because of a personal loyalty to somebody. Deep inside us, we knew we were not going anywhere. We knew we faced eventual defeat."

★　★　★

Marcos was awake the whole night. What else was left for him to do, with Enrile demanding that he step down from the presidency? Washington, although it had stated a policy against direct involvement when the revolution began, was beginning to pressure him into giving up. Reagan had called the previous day to advise him that his time was up and that he, his family, and his associates would be welcome to live in the United States. Before that, Reagan had warned Marcos against the use of military force in order to remain in power. That was on Day 1, but although Marcos had ordered his troops to assault Camp Crame several times on Days 2 and 3 and had thus ignored Reagan, actually no attack was carried out. Marcos' hand was so far unsmeared by blood and, therefore, he still qualified for Reagan's offer of sanctuary.

It can be assumed that Marcos, in the first hours of Day 4, had realized that he had lost the support of the armed forces. In Malacañang, he was in the same situation that Enrile and Ramos were at the start of the revolution: holed up in a static defense position that had no chance of standing up to a massive blow. Denied offensive military capability, Marcos informed Fort Bonifacio to ignore all previous orders to attack.

His mind relieved of military problems, Marcos concentrated his thoughts on his potential future. Could he compromise by sharing power with his opponents? Was there such a thing as stepping down a little bit and holding on to some vestige of power?

★ ★ ★

Marcos' telephone rang. It was Minister of Labor and Employment Blas Ople reporting from the American capital. He had been sent on a mission to Washington just after the February 7 elections to show the Americans that Marcos had won the presidential race, contrary to reports from some sectors of the press that Mrs. Aquino was the legitimate winner. Ople reported on a meeting he had just had with Secretary of State George Shultz and Undersecretary of State for Political Affairs Michael Armacost. Ople said the State Department assessment of the Philippine situation was this: Marcos had lost control of the armed forces; the troops left with Ver were impotent; Marcos should step down or there would be civil war. The report angered Marcos; he did not expect the Americans would do this to a friend, and abandon him in the face of peril and tell him what to do, which in effect was suicide. Ople heard him say that Mrs. Marcos was against leaving the country.

Marcos could not understand why Reagan had let him down. Shortly after the elections, the American President had issued a statement that he felt both sides did not have clean hands when it came to election frauds. Then followed a statement that the election frauds were "perpetrated overwhelmingly by the ruling party" so as to put a cloud over the legitimacy of the continued rule of Marcos. Then the State Department released a statement in Reagan's name urging Marcos to resign. Ambassador Bosworth had sent a copy of this statement to Malacañang.

★ ★ ★

At 1 a.m., Marcos picked up the telephone and asked to be connected with Nevada Republican Senator Paul Laxalt, a friend and confidant of Reagan, in Washington, D.C., who had headed the team of observers that visited the Philippines before and during the elections.

Marcos told Laxalt he wanted to know the latest thinking of Reagan on the Philippine situation and he alluded to the State Department message. "I'd like to know whether this is valid," Marcos said.

"It is," Laxalt replied. He gave a brief backgrounder on the statement, coupled with troubleshooter Ambassador Philip Habib's latest report on the military and political aspects of the Enrile-Ramos breakaway.

Then Marcos said he thought an arrangement could be found whereby he would share power with the opposition. He was thinking of a provisional government to last until 1987, when his term would expire. By then, a viable constitutional regime would have been established. In the meantime, he would be helping solve the provisional government's problems of countryside insurgency and finances.

Laxalt gave Marcos his personal view that power-sharing would not work. He asked Marcos to wait while he consulted Reagan.

While Marcos was talking with Laxalt, Mrs. Marcos called up Mrs. Nancy Reagan asking for her intercession with the U.S. President to give Marcos a break. Mrs. Reagan said she would consult her husband and let Mrs. Marcos know what he said.

Laxalt came back to the phone and told Marcos that Reagan agreed with the view that power-sharing would be impractical and reiterated the assurance that Marcos and his retinue would be welcome in the United States.

"But the Philippines is my home," Marcos pleaded. "I want to stay and die here." He confided his worry about harassment by the U.S. Congress should he be on American territory. Laxalt assured him that would not be any problem.

Mrs. Reagan returned the call of Mrs. Marcos and told her she would be welcome in the United States and Marcos probably knew by that time what was in Reagan's mind.

★ ★ ★

United States reaction to the events unfolding in the Philippines, while guarded at the start, definitely encouraged the Enrile-Ramos rebellion, and helped hasten the erosion of support, particularly by the Philippine military, of the Marcos regime.

On Day 1 of the revolution, the White House issued a statement which in effect affirmed one of the reasons given by Enrile and Ramos for their breakaway with Marcos: the rigging of the elections by the Marcos ruling party which thwarted the will of the electorate. The statement called for a peaceful resolution of the conflict and stopped short of endorsing the rebellion. But it denounced Marcos for the electoral fraud which it noted was "so extreme as to undermine the credibility and legitimacy of the election and impair the capacity of the government to cope with a growing insurgency and troubled economy."

Marcos' critics on Capitol Hill also quickly joined the fray. Sen. Richard Lugar, chairman of the powerful Senate Foreign Relations Committee who headed an observer team here during the elections, said on the first day of the revolt: "President Marcos will have to face the reality. He has lost the Church, he has lost the middle class, and clearly, he is now in the process of losing the military support." He added, "All our aid has been directed toward these reform-minded officers, literally to bring about efficiency of the army. Our hope always was with General Ramos and the younger officers, to bring about a spirit of reform."

Rep. Stephen Solarz, chairman of the House Subcommittee on Asian Affairs and archcritic of Marcos in the US, was more direct and, in the end, prophetic. He said, "Saturday's revolt could obviously be the beginning of the end of the Marcos regime."

Sen. John Kerry, a member of the Lugar observer team, had this to say about the outbreak of the military rebellion against Marcos:". . . Hopefully Marcos will come to see the writing on the wall and there will be a peaceful transition of power. There's no question that Cory Aquino is the rightfutlly elected President of the Philippines."

As the revolution progressed into its second and third day, US reaction became increasingly and pointedly for the Enrile-Ramos camp. History is yet to judge the extent of America's contribution to the success of the revolution.

★ ★ ★

At 3 a.m., Marcos again called Laxalt. He sounded like a boy lost in the woods. He had a question for Laxalt to answer.

Laxalt asked Marcos if he had been up all night. And Marcos said yes, because he was afraid the Palace would be stormed.

"Senator, what do you think? Marcos asked. "Should I step down? What should I do?"

Laxalt replied curtly: "I think you should cut. And cut cleanly. I think the time has come."

Marcos was speechless for a few minutes.

"Mr. President, are you still there?" Laxalt asked.

"Yes," Marcos answered in a pained voice. "I'm so very, very disappointed."

★ ★ ★

Marcos still had one card to play. He could sell the power-sharing idea to Enrile.

He waited for morning.

★ ★ ★

At 3:30 a.m., the Marines at Fort Bonifacio were jubilant over the news that Marcos had just cancelled his order for them to attack Camp Crame using six mortars. They had been worried because they were just about ready to defect to the rebel side.

At 3:45 a.m., two RF-27 and two C-130 planes used as troop transports took off from Villamor Air Base on a mission of ferrying reinforcements ordered by Ver. The pilots changed flight plans and landed at Clark where they would be frozen for the duration of the revolution. Pilots at Basa Air Base did the same thing with five T-33s, 10 F5s, and seven F8s. The C-130 from Legazpi City that carried troops to augment the security of the Manila International Airport also flew to Clark. The 5th Fighter Wing and the 220th Heavy Airlift Wing thus completed their transfer, lock, stock, and barrel, to the rebel side.

★ ★ ★

Task Force Delta continued its campaign to place all radio and television stations within the jurisdiction of the rebels. Delta with reinforcements from Camp Crame were led by Lt. Col. Rodolfo Aguinaldo in an assault on the Channel 9 transmitter in Broadcast City. Snipers atop the tower were harassing the people and troops in the vicinity of Channel 4. By 2:30 p.m., the transmitter was crippled, three of the defending troops were killed and one wounded. An attempt was made by Ver's forces to retake Channel 9, but their approach was blocked by human barricades. Before that, Ver's troops had tried to take Channel 7 but were frustrated by human barricades surrounding the place. The troops who belonged to the 14th Infantry Battalion simply joined the rebels.

Even so, Ver was not giving up on his efforts to retake the television and radio stations despite a warning sent to him from Washington hinting that he would not be allowed to leave with Marcos if he did not freeze his troops. Brawner was worried that his Rangers would again be utilized to get hold of as many stations as possible for Marcos' inaugural ceremonies at noon. Brawner was called by Kanapi to report to Army headquarters at Fort Bonifacio. Suspecting that there would be another mission for the Rangers, Brawner did not respond. Instead, he prepared to report to Camp Crame.

★ ★ ★

The Marines agreed on a conditional loyalty to Marcos. They would protect him from attackers but would refuse to fight in a situation where civilians would be hurt. Tadiar saw Ver at the Community Hall to convey their position. Tadiar observed that Ver was sad, "I fully understand your position," Ver told him. "Anyway, thank you for being frank and straightforward with me." Before they parted, Ver told Tadiar to take good care of himself. That was the last time they saw each other.

★ ★ ★

At Camp Crame, Enrile and Ramos were preparing to go to the Club Filipino for the inauguration of Mrs. Aquino as President and Salvador Laurel as Vice President.

The telephone rang. It was Marcos asking for Enrile. The conversation ran thus:

Marcos — I am looking for a graceful way out. Am thinking of cancelling the election, thus continuing with my term as President until 1987. I would remain merely as honorary President while you would be head of a provisional government. You can then run the government in any manner you want.

Enrile — Mr. President, it was never my intention nor the intention of my group to assume power. Our main intention was merely to see to it that the will of our people must be respected. And besides, it is now too late even to discuss any arrangements because we have already committed ourselves to Cory and Doy.

Marcos — Would you kindly discuss this anyway with your group, and maybe, with Mrs. Aquino, and maybe, find a solution to the problem?

Enrile — I see no need for such discussion. But I'll see if it is possible.

Marcos — Could I possibly live in the Philippines?

Enrile — We have no aggressive intentions against the First Family. I can assure you, Mr. President, that as far as my group and I are concerned, you will always be protected if you want to live in the Philippines.

Marcos — If I go abroad, do you think I can safely come back here?

Enrile — Of course, you can come and go as you wish.

Marcos — How about the safety of General Ver?

Enrile — That is something I cannot answer. I cannot guarantee the attitude of the young officers regarding him.

Marcos — Can you try to explore these issues? Kindly call me back.

Enrile — I'll try.

After the conversation, Enrile and Ramos took a helicopter to the inauguration site about five kilometers away. They were wearing their usual working clothes with the revolutionary insignia indicating the fourth day of the Revolution.

★ ★ ★

The ceremonies did not have the glitter one would expect of a lavish inauguration. Mrs. Aquino was in a simple yellow dress and Laurel in ordinary barong Pilipino. Nobody was in formal wear. A limited crowd of around 2,000 packed the clubhouse.

The two officials were sworn in by Supreme Court Justice Claudio Teehankee.

"On the basis of the people's mandate clearly manifested last February 7, I and Salvador H. Laurel are taking power in the name and by the will of the Filipino people as President and Vice President, respectively," Mrs. Aquino declared.

The first appointments made by President Aquino, and these she announced right after the inauguration ceremonies, were those of Enrile as minister of national defense and Ramos as chief of staff of the New Armed Forces of the Philippines.

After the ceremonies, Enrile and Ramos flew back to Camp Crame. Later, they proceeded to make a ceremonial occupation of Camp Aguinaldo for the New Armed Forces of the Philippines. Ramos occupied the office of the chief of staff. Enrile went back to the work room in which he had dedicated 16 years of his life.

★ ★ ★

Both armed camps were more relaxed now. The bloody skirmish at Channel 9 was not expected to provoke any escalation of fighting. It was going to be self-limiting because of its specific objective. Fort Bonifacio appeared to have lost its initiative and the modus vivendi secretly arranged by Abadia with Camp Crame gave cause for the people manning the fort to take it easy.

Suddenly, the simmering tension came to boiling point in a sector of Fort Bonifacio, when a colonel received information that a unit of the 14th Infantry Battalion had been attacked by two Sikorskys. The colonel immediately rang up an Academy classmate at operations in Camp Crame.

"What's this I hear about your heli strike on the 14th IB?" the colonel shouted. "Those are my boys!"

"We are not attacking anyone. Relax," was the reply.

"Remember, if anyone of my boys get hurt, I have howitzers

here. You should honor your word, Cavalier."

"I said relax. The only air mission we had in that sector was a leaflet drop. I'm sure your boys read the message."

On the other hand, at Camp Crame, there was alarm over a report that a 15-tank column from the north was rolling into Manila. This prompted Sotelo's pilots to go up on a search-and-destroy mission. It turned out to be a false alarm.

In Cotabato, Gutang was still worrying about Bibit and the constables he sent to join Ramos but were captured by the Aviation Security Command upon landing at the MIA. Bibit and his group at this time were in a detention center in Fort Bonifacio planning how to escape. They complained of rough handling during their arrest and pilferage of personal belongings by their guards. Bibit complained he was too tightly handcuffed and an enlisted man came to tighten the handcuffs further. Gutang sent a rescue team led by Major Santos to Fort Bonifacio but it arrived when Bibit and his group were already set free after announcement of the fall of Marcos.

★ ★ ★

J. P. Laurel street (named after the father of Mrs. Aquino's running mate) was teeming with Marcos' own version of people power. The narrow street, built back in the days of the Spanish colonial government, was teeming with Marcos followers from Nagtahan bridge to Ayala bridge with placards and banners bearing the campaign slogan, "*Marcos pa rin!*" (It's still Marcos!) There were about 2,000 in the street and more than a thousand in the Palace grounds where coffee and sandwiches were available. Most of the people had been there since the night Marcos appealed on television for their help. As noontime approached, about a thousand more joined the pro-Marcos barricades. At Gate 4, a man with a bullhorn welcomed all vehicles and persons coming for the inauguration ceremonies. There were reports that some of them were stoned by pro-Aquino groups on the way to Malacañang.

Presidential security men were edgy. Somebody in the crowd exploded a firecracker and a soldier was so quick on the draw he fired and hurt an Army lieutenant and eight civilians, among them Melinda Liu of *Newsweek*, who was there covering the event.

★ ★ ★

Mendiola, a road of about 200 meters connecting J. P. Laurel and Legarda streets, was also filled with Marcos followers up to the point where barbed-wire accordions several meters deep cut it off from Legarda. A pro-Aquino crowd of over a thousand at this portion of Legarda were eyeing the soldiers guarding that point, and each side was beginning to taunt the other. Mendiola was the road from which a mob had attempted to break into Malacañang in 1972, prompting Marcos to declare martial law.

A reporter who entered Malacañang at 11:15 a.m. saw only five other members of the Press Corps and a few foreign newsmen there. He saw about 5,000 people in front of the stage outside Maharlika Hall. Less than a thousand were allowed to enter the Palace, and only half of them were permitted to be in the Ceremonial Hall where Marcos was to take his oath of office.

Among the high officials who came were Minister of Tourism Jose D. Aspiras, Agrarian Reform Minister Conrado Estrella, Agriculture Minister Salvador Escudero III, Food Administrator Jesus Tanchanco, Information Minister Cendaña, Public Works Minister Jesus Hipolito, Deputy Minister Aber Canlas, Education Minister Jaime Laya, Minister Juan Tuvera, MP Antonio Raquiza, MP Arturo Pacificador, MP Salvador Brittanico, MP Rodolfo del Rosario, MP Manuel Collantes, former Senator Rodolfo Ganzon and Justice Buenaventura Guerrero. Many wondered why Vice President-elect Arturo Tolentino, Prime Minister Cesar Virata, and Trade Minister Roberto Ongpin were not there.

The only generals present were Ver, Edon Yap, Barangan, Zumel, and Ochoco. Col. Dioscoro E. Yoro, Jr., a former aide and close friend of Marcos (but an enemy of Ver) held a Sterling submachinegun. In 1975, Ver gave Yoro a field assignment to separate him from Marcos. Yoro claimed Ver was jealous.

Piccio was not there because he was at Villamor Air Base advising personnel they were free to take sides but they must avoid bloodshed.

Ramas was in Fort Bonifacio, reportedly to tell his associates to follow their conscience if they felt the urge to move to the other side. Earlier that day, Ramas had a visitor in the person of Ambassador Rafael Ileto, former Armed Forces vice chief of staff. Ileto had been requested by Enrile to talk with the generals on the other side of the conflict and persuade them to defect. Apparently, the top brass, even before Marcos took his oath, had heard from the grapevine that their Chief was leaving the country.

★ ★ ★

At 11:45 a.m., the Marcoses entered the half-filled Ceremonial Hall. They were greeted with cheers of, "Marcos, Marcos, Marcos pa rin!" Marcos was in barong Pilipino; Mrs. Marcos, Imee, and Irene wore white ternos. The ladies were dewy-eyed but managed to smile and appear radiant. Tommy Manotoc and Greggy Araneta were also there. Of Marcos' only son, reporter Alex Allan observed: "I looked at Bongbong's face. His chin is quivering. His fists are clenching and unclenching. He looks for all the world like a young man in anguish who does not want to give up, who wants to strike at something or somebody for his father."

Allan later wrote: "Recalling the scene again and reviewing young Bongbong's reactions, I should have guessed then that the President had already made a decision to leave the country after his telephone conversation early that morning with Senator Paul Laxalt and, afterwards, with Minister Ponce Enrile. It is my guess now that he communicated that decision to the First Lady, his son, and Ver, but not to his two daughters."

Lito Gorospe was master of ceremonies. The national anthem was sung. Fr. Domingo Nebres and three other ministers recited the invocation.

Marcos stood behind the podium. Chief Justice Ramon C. Aquino, who was called to spend the night in the Palace so as to assure his presence, swore him into office as President at 11:55 a.m.

Marcos had barely taken his oath when Channel 9, which covered the event, was cut off the air. It had just been taken by Task Force Delta.

Marcos read a brief speech. "No man can be more proud than I am at this moment," he said. He mentioned something about hitting back at the rebels. There was not much out of the text of that inaugural address that the newsmen cared to pick up. The ritual was over in 20 minutes, then Chief Justice Aquino was called back to reenact the oathtaking for movie cameras and video cassette tapes. Everybody appeared in a hurry to go home, the high officials especially. Cendaña appeared no longer interested in treating newsmen to lunch; he simply dropped out of sight.

The crowd near Marcos shouted invectives at the rebels, then they broke into applause and chanted, "Marcos, Marcos, Marcos pa rin!" They waved small Philippine flags.

Marcos, followed by his wife and son, headed towards a balcony, shaking hands with guests along the way. At the balcony, they waved to the crowd gathered down below. Cameramen took pictures of them from the improvised stage on which the oathtaking had been intended to take place, but had to be moved indoors for security reasons.

From the balcony, Marcos delivered a strongly worded speech in Pilipino. He was cheered every time his fighting mood took a peak. The crowd chanted, "Martial law, martial law!"

Newsmen stopped Ver briefly as he walked across the hall. He was asked about his plans. He replied, smiling, "We have not fired a single shot." He appeared less worried than Mrs. Marcos.

★ ★ ★

The Marcoses retired to their quarters. By mid-afternoon the Palace was empty. Rumors flew thick and fast the Marcoses would be leaving that day.

But hundreds of Marcos followers remained to barricade the streets outside the Palace. Those on Mendiola street went into a stone-throwing battle with the pro-Aquino crowd on Legarda, but this was stopped by the Police. At J. P. Laurel and Nagtahan, hundreds of pro-Marcos people waving small flags replaced the bulk of uniformed troops. They even occupied the overpass across Magsaysay boulevard.

★ ★ ★

Over at Camp Crame, people power did not ebb. Although Mrs. Aquino had been inaugurated as President, concern remained for the rebels and the New Armed Forces of the Philippines that had now become the backbone of national stability and security. Human barricades went up around the newly acquired radio and television stations and in every strategic place that could spell a possible attack on Crame. In Metropolitan Manila, this unarmed civilian army of men, women, and children of all walks of life was estimated at 800,000. Some estimates went as far as a million. They were fed from donations given by businessmen, professionals, and civic and religious organizations. They were driven to that point of sacrifice by their desire to oust Marcos and bring an end to his regime of two long decades. They were encouraged by the possibility that Enrile, Ramos, and the Reformists would succeed in forcing Marcos out of power. They had seen no other combination of moral and military force pitted against Marcos all these years of suffering. Now, at last, they saw deliverance was at hand.

★ ★ ★

Defections continued on Day 4 of the Revolution. A reception area was established at the Crame grandstand to usher soldiers of all ranks into the New Armed Forces. Ramos received Brawner and his entire Ranger regiment. Officers and men of Piccio streamed in. Army and naval officers and men. Many of them were practically pushed in by relatives at the barricades. Ramos revealed that Olivas had been on his side since Day 1 but the information had to be kept under wraps to deceive Marcos. When Marcos suspected on Day 3 that Olivas was with Ramos, he appointed Victor Natividad chief of Constabulary and director general of the Integrated National Police. Olivas retired from the service when Mrs. Aquino assumed office as President. Ramos then named Brig. Gen. Renato de Villa as chief of PC and director general of the Integrated National Police. It has been said of the PC that on Day 4, there were three Constabulary chiefs, De Villa, Natividad, and Olivas, because Olivas never relinquished his Marcos-given command to Natividad.

At 4 p.m., Marcos called Enrile and this was their conversation.

Marcos — Will you please order your men to stop firing at the Palace?

Enrile — Mr. President, I have no people in that area.

Marcos — Who are these people then?

Enrile — It is possible that they are provocateurs trying to aggravate the situation.

Marcos — Then will you please send a detachment to investigate and stop the firing?

After a while, Marcos made this request:

Marcos — Johnny, will you kindly contact Ambassador

Bosworth and ask him if he could assign Brig. Gen. Teddy Allen of JUSMAG and his men to provide a security escort for me to get out of the Palace?

★ ★ ★

While Marcos and Enrile were talking, ranking officers at the Community Hall waited on the other side of the river. Among them were Ochoco, Pattugalan, Zumel, Varona, Colonel Ochoco, and Colonel Ver. Marcos' chief of staff was in his quarters. At 4 p.m., Ver, in civilian attire, joined the group at the Community Hall. It is probable he told them he was leaving with the First Family. An observer noted he looked wan and helpless.

At 5 p.m., Ver was called by Marcos. He and son Irwin crossed the river and went to the Palace, then he rejoined his friends at the Community Hall.

Apparently, only the officers at the hall knew what was going on. No other military personnel had any inkling of Marcos' impending departure. Themselves in the dark, the escort officers of the Marcoses went into a huddle and discussed their own contingency plans. They saw household employees packing — bags, boxes, suitcases belonging to the Marcoses. Then Greggy Araneta asked the escort officers to sound out their men for volunteers to accompany the Marcoses should they decide to leave the Palace. Capt. Nestor Sadiarin and seven men volunteered. But the mission was soon forgotten. It was said that Marcos wanted to go home to Ilocos Norte on the northwestern tip of Luzon; he refused to leave the Philippines, although his daughters were begging him to change his mind. It is reported that he had to be sedated so that he could be carried out of the Palace, but this cannot be confirmed.

★ ★ ★

The American embassy acted with dispatch on Marcos' request, conveyed through Enrile, for General Allen to provide the means of transportation out of the Palace. The embassy notified the Palace of arrangements at 7 p.m. The US embassy gave the Marcoses two hours to leave the palace. Marcos called Ver again to his study. Ver went alone, after giving instructions to his sons, Irwin, Wyrlo, and Rexor, to meet him there.

His duty escort, Lt. Leopoldo D. Morante, Jr., could not forget his parting words: "Lt. Morante, thank you for all the services you have rendered me, my family, and the armed forces. Carry on." The young officer went straight home to sleep and forget those four harried days of the revolution.

When Ver saw Marcos, he was told of a report that the Marines were about to storm the Palace. Actually, there was no such threat, but instead of verifying the information, Ver held his arms up, then struck his right fist into his left palm, as if in desperation. Mrs. Marcos cried on her husband's shoulder. Marcos comforted her.

★ ★ ★

At 7:30 p.m., two American helicopters from Clark touched down on the Pangarap golf course at Malacañang Park. The evacuation operations went smoothly. Marcos and his family took the first helicopter, Ver and his sons the second. Some belongings were ferried to the US embassy on a small boat to be taken from there to Clark. Half an hour later, two other helicopters landed at Pangarap and picked up the rest of the Marcos retinue.

The families of Ver and his sons, Ambassador Eduardo Cojuangco and his family motored to Clark that night to join the Marcos party.

★ ★ ★

As the last American chopper lifted off the ground, the crowd on Mendiola which had turned into a mob surged through Gate 4 and occupied Malacañang. Some of them occupied the administration building and the palace and went on a looting spree.

Some of the angry crowd caught a number of security men and members of the palace household loading ten pieces of luggage and other valuables belonging to the First Family into a rubber boat behind the palace that would take them to the US embassy compound via the Pasig River where another American chopper was to pick them up.

The security men and the household members had to jump into the murky Pasig River to avoid the mob. Luckily, not one of them drowned. The luggage containing money, jewelry, documents, and other valuables were looted right on the spot. Not one of the looters, however, was able to enter the palace as security men had locked the main entrance leading to the rooms and offices of the President and the First Lady and their children.

Meanwhile, the looters at the administration building stripped clean the offices of Minister Cendaña on the third floor, including the office of his special executive assistant and disbursing officer who lost cash, important documents, and other valuables.

As the looting progressed into the night, another crowd of over 3,000 breached the security perimeter of the Malacañang Park's Sector III across the Pasig River where Marcos and his party boarded the choppers and looted the whole area, including the Presidential Guard armory. Over 1,000 Galil's, Uzis, armalites, and handguns were taken by the looters from the Park, the Palace, and the administration building.

★ ★ ★

Marcos and his party of 100 persons arrived at Clark Air Force Base at 9:30 p.m. They were met by officers of the Office of Special Investigation (OSI), led by Col. Robert Cuniff; Col. Kenneth Fadel, chief of the Security Police Group (American), and other ranking officers. No

Filipinos, civilian or military, were present from the time of landing to the departure of the Marcos party from Clark. However, information gathered by the Philippine government indicated that members of the Marcos party and their luggage were subjected to a more or less thorough search at Clark. Their luggage were scanned by X-ray and subsequently inspected. All the firearms in their possession or stashed in their luggage were either surrendered to or confiscated by the American military authorities.

Among the significant items in the possession of the Marcoses, aside from a big number of high-powered and low-caliber firearms, were two gold crowns and other items of gold contained in a pullman-size black bag. This bag was not among those seen loaded in the aircraft that flew the Marcoses to Guam.

Also inventoried as part of the Marcos possessions were Philippine peso bills amounting to ₱26.3 million, and US$3 million. Oddly, Clark authorities allowed the Marcoses to bring with them to the US only the Philippine money.

Another suitcase with no identifying marks on it contained jewelry of "high value," mostly diamonds. A maroon briefcase in the name of Alex Ganut, a member of the party, had the figure "P122" taped outside, and contained money. Three suitcases contained assorted fur coats, obviously belonging to Mrs. Marcos and her two daughters.

The Marcoses also brought a lot of video tape cassettes (VHS) with them. Clark authorities counted some 200 such VHS tapes.

The Marcos papers were contained in several suitcases, but one in particular caught the attention of the base officials. Marked "F. Marcos," it contained old copies of "sex magazines," as they were described.

The evening was spent preparing for the trip to Guam. The Marcoses were billeted at the Chambers Hall. Two planes were readied for the trip, a C-9 paramedic aircraft for the ailing President and his family, and a C-141 Starlifter for the rest of the party.

★ ★ ★

At 3 a.m., the President was awakened and asked to prepare for the trip to Guam. The man who imagined himself, since the days of his youth, to be an invincible Maharlika, or one destined to lead, had been proved by the four-day revolution as destined to leave.

★ ★ ★

At 5 a.m., February 26, 1986, the C-9 bearing the President took off from Clark Air Force Base and out of Philippine soil. ☐

CHAPTER V

"I could be the only defense minister in the entire world who is under surveillance by his own government."

— Enrile

SEEDS OF THE REVOLUTION

As spontaneous as the outburst that it was, the revolution did not really happen overnight. It was the culmination of a decade of popular disenchantment with a ruler who didn't know when to stop, not even when Benigno Aquino who had come home to claim his place among his people was brutally murdered before he could set foot on his native land. The revolution was bred in widespread privation and poverty as much as the shameless extravagance of a few. Millions were condemned to a life of hopelessness and despair as the economy sank and the specter of graft and corruption grew larger than life.

Inevitably, the revolution was a clash of personalities who, like characters in a stage play, were playing out their roles as history blocked their positions like a crafty director. The cast: Minister of National Defense Juan Ponce Enrile and Armed Forces Vice Chief of Staff, Lt. General Fidel V. Ramos. The political Opposition led by then presidential candidate Corazon C. Aquino. The Catholic clergy headed by Jaime Cardinal Sin. An unlikely alliance of forces joining hands to break the back of Ferdinand Marcos and his henchman, General Fabian Ver.

★ ★ ★

Of all the characters in that drama at EDSA, the roles played by Enrile and Ramos deserve to be placed in perspective. Neither man was a reason for the popular discontent that grew under Marcos; they were, in fact, among the most disenchanted. But when the time came for them to dramatize their discontent, it was the military that turned the tide against Marcos. That role, as skillfully choreographed by Enrile and Ramos, cannot be overestimated. Corazon Aquino may have won the elections, but if the military had not intervened as it did in shifting loyalty from the dictator to Enrile and Ramos, there is serious doubt if she could have effectively claimed the presidency for herself. Marcos may have been as bad and as hopelessly unpopular as he had been pictured to be, and he may have truly robbed Mrs. Aquino of her election, but if he had retained the loyalty of the military, Mrs. Aquino's emotional campaign would have stayed in the wings a long, long time before anyone could even think of driving out Marcos.

But when the military, harking to Enrile and Ramos, decided to intervene, and whole units and entire commands of the armed forces started transferring their loyalty to Ramos and Enrile all night of February 22 and throughout February 23 and 24, Marcos was exposed in all his nakedness — a leader with no followers, a strongman without an army to enforce his will, a loser whose only escape was flight from the wrath of his people.

Other elements in the defense and military establishment were acting out their own part of the drama that was to have its climax on EDSA. Their objectives were the same as those of the "parliament of the streets" — indefatigable, incorrigible marchers, rallyists, demonstrators. They differed only in their orientation and approaches. The military reformists were fighting for changes from within the system. They perceived the degeneration of the regime, and the military organization along with it. They realized that as a consequence, the military was losing the support of the people, who were essential in the fight against insurgency. They wanted to stop the infamy that the military uniform had unwittingly created in the eyes and minds of the civilian populace. They wanted to be able to wear their uniforms with pride and dignity once again.

In a series of appearances before the nation and before the world while holed up at Camp Aguinaldo and Camp Crame, Enrile and Ramos gave the reasons for their disenchantment with their Commander-in-Chief. They spoke of how their differences with the then First Lady, Mrs. Imelda Romualdez Marcos, with General Fabian C. Ver, then armed forces chief of staff, and with President Marcos himself as the willing ally of Mrs. Marcos and General Ver, had resulted in the erosion of their influence over the military which stymied their efforts to introduce reforms. They told of how their authority was undermined, how they were bypassed in the decision-making process, how they had become, in their own words, mere "deodorants" to cover the stink of the rotten Marcos regime.

In Enrile's case, the reason for the disenchantment started on a parochial note. As leader of the Cagayan region in the northern part of the country, he had tried to develop and assert his leadership. But for reasons that would surface later, Mrs. Marcos and General Ver, with tacit encouragement from Mr. Marcos, tried to undermine his leadership by propping up his political opponents.

There was another reason. Because of his achievements and successes as minister of defense, and before that, as commissioner of customs, secretary of finance and secretary of justice, all Cabinet positions under Marcos, Enrile's popularity had soared and he had become a logical contender for the presidency. This put him on a collision course with the First Lady, the most powerful and most influential person in the government, next only to the President, who had her sights trained on the highest office.

★ ★ ★

Shortly after the declaration of martial law in 1972, it was Enrile whom Marcos instructed to handle media control and enforce the travel ban on Filipinos going abroad. One day after he received the instructions, Enrile got a call from Mrs. Marcos at the Central Bank building on Roxas Boulevard where he was attending a Cabinet meeting. Mrs. Marcos was requesting a travel clearance for the daughter-in-law of former Sen. Raul S. Manglapus who wanted to join her husband in Tokyo. The minister said yes.

★ ★ ★

The next day, the woman's mother went to Enrile's office to get the clearance Mrs. Marcos had requested. After interviewing the woman, the minister learned that the daughter would be coming from Tokyo to deliver her baby here and then go back to Tokyo.

Since the travel clearance was not for an urgent or life-or-death reason, and fearing that he might be accused of discrimination, Enrile declined to give her the clearance. The mother complained to the First Lady.

In the evening, the minister was summoned to attend a meeting with the President, General Espino, and other top officials. Just before the meeting started, the phone rang. It was for Enrile. An irate First Lady was on the other end of the line. She had a few angry words for his ear: "You are swell-headed, arrogant, and cocky!"

Enrile tried to explain that he was merely following government regulations, but Mrs. Marcos would not have it: "I don't care about regulations! You know, I am going to destroy you."

"If you think I am a liability, why don't you tell the President to allow me to leave the Cabinet?" Enrile replied.

"Don't threaten me with resignation!" Mrs. Marcos yelled and slammed the phone.

At the meeting, Enrile recounted the incident to the President.

"That's the trouble with Imelda; she doesn't know what's happening," the President said, sounding apologetic.

A few days later, Enrile refused yet another would-be traveler, the millionaire-businessman Virgilio Hilario, who would be leaving with his wife, the former Miss Universe, Armi Kuusela. A complaint reached the First Lady but this time, she did not call the minister.

★ ★ ★

As signs that Mrs. Marcos did not approve, the issuance of travel clearances and the control of the media were removed from Enrile and transferred to the Office of the President. Presidential Executive Assistant Guillermo de Vega took over the issuance of travel clearances while newsman Primitivo Mijares handled the media.

A systematic sowing of intrigues by Mrs. Marcos designed to oust Enrile soon became apparent. One day, Col. Francisco Romualdez, elder stepbrother of the First Lady, showed up at Enrile's office at Camp Aguinaldo. Romualdez informed Enrile of talk going on in Malacañang that Enrile was going to be replaced.

"Why not, if that's the desire of the President?" Enrile retorted. Romualdez left.

After that, Mrs. Marcos started ignoring Enrile, whether at Palace functions, during Cabinet meetings or in social gatherings.

Even the Minister's wife, Cristina, who was one of the original Blue Ladies frequently in the company of the First Lady, was ignored. Actually, Mrs. Enrile welcomed the snub. She has always been known as a simple woman who would rather stay out of the social limelight if she could help it. She reacted by also ignoring Mrs. Marcos.

From that time onward, she never set foot in Malacañang.

★ ★ ★

As martial law dragged on, Mrs. Marcos, with the help of General Ver, worked out a plan to destroy Enrile in his own turf. Destroy him locally, and he is kaput nationally.

The first test came in May 1978, shortly before the election for the Interim Batasang Pambansa or parliament. Enrile was a candidate for the lone Batasan seat in his home province of Cagayan. The First Lady and General Ver were determined to stop him in his tracks.

One day during the campaign, Enrile was summoned to Malacañang and asked to declassify and make public the intelligence files of the defense ministry linking former Sen. Benigno S. Aquino, Jr. to the U.S. Central Intelligence Agency (CIA). The idea was to deglamorize Aquino, who was fighting the First Lady in Manila's Batasan polls. Aquino and Mrs. Marcos were at the head of opposing tickets in the drive for the premier legislative assembly seats in the capital region of Metropolitan Manila.

Enrile did as he was told. But in the middle of the exposé on Aquino's CIA connection, the late senator was allowed by the President to go on TV. From his cell at Fort Bonifacio, the imprisoned opposition leader pulled the rug from under Enrile and admitted his links with the CIA in the 1950's.

Embarassed and feeling awkward by the open admission, Enrile decided not to pursue the issue. But he had sensed that Marcos had had a part in the script to undermine Enrile's credibility, and perhaps Marcos had done so at the prodding of the First Lady.

Enrile flew to Cagayan to resume his campaign. He won by an overwhelming majority.

★ ★ ★

In Metro Manila, the Kilusang Bagong Lipunan (New Society Movement) crushed the Aquino ticket, 21-0, amid charges of massive vote-buying and terrorism by the ruling party.

Meanwhile, peace and order suffered a setback and the insurgency problem was spreading so alarmingly that even urban centers had become targets of attack.

In November of 1978, Enrile went to Dolores, Samar, after a week in Mindanao and Palawan, to check out the peace and order there. Two days before the trip, he had received a report that a PC unit had shot it out with Navy construction battalion troopers at the airport.

Upon his arrival in Dolores, Enrile called a meeting with town officials and residents, during which he learned that the Navy men had provoked the Constabulary troopers. Enrile relieved the entire Navy contingent. A plane flew them out. When Enrile returned to Manila, there was a call from the President asking him to report to Malacañang.

"You have no command authority to relieve the Navy contingent," the President told the defense chief. Enrile tried to reason out but the President was sore.

"Forget it," the President told Enrile later, but Marcos was not one to forget. Shortly afterwards, he issued Letter of Instructions No. 776 divesting Enrile and then Armed Forces chief of staff General Romeo C. Espino of authority to relieve, reassign, or promote military personnel. The LOI was not for general circulation; it was "for limited eyes only."

It read:

> "In line with the continuing program of reforms in the government, I hereby order the following:
>
> "Review of the assignment of senior officers of the Armed Forces of the Philippines, which will include a determination of

their qualifications and performance and a review of their past records and activities, derogatory or otherwise; and

"No change of assignment of senior officers, including provincial commanders, brigade commanders and division commanders
and special unit commanders, shall be made without prior clearance from the President."

The first two paragraphs were just a cover. The President, in
Paragraph 3, betrayed his real intention. Enrile and Espino had been
recommending the relief and transfer of some commanders for abuses
in the field. But their recommendations fell on deaf ears. Enrile saw the
hand of the First Lady and General Ver behind the issuance of LOI
776.

★ ★ ★

A rumor was also traced to Mrs. Marcos and General Ver to the
effect that Enrile was establishing his political base in the Cagayan Valley in order to challenge Marcos in the presidential election of 1981.
The rumors were meant to filter down to the KBL ranks. The objective
was to make the defense minister look like an opportunist out to grab
the presidency.

Certain now of formidable enemies in the Palace, Enrile began to
keep to himself, avoiding even the reporters covering and travelling
frequently to his province.

In the flurry of the campaign, the President made several pro-
nouncements, prominent among which was the replacement of
mayors all over the country, especially those with pending cases
against them. Seven mayors of Cagayan were affected — those in Tu-
ao, Buguey, Iguig, Amulong, Claveria, Solana, and Gattaran. Enrile
consulted Governor Teresa Dupaya, wife of his political arch rival,
Tito Dupaya. An agreement was reached, but it was shortlived. Enrile
learned of underhanded efforts to subvert it. For instance, the First

Lady's younger brother, Benjamin "Kokoy" Romualdez, tried to stop the replacement of Buguey Mayor Licerio Antiporda, a Dupaya boy, although Marcos had already appointed Jorge Arriola on Enrile's recommendation.

A meeting to thresh out the problem was held at Alfredo's restaurant in Quezon City, attended by Antiporda and the Dupayas. Antiporda was in Cagayan that day but "Kokoy" had him fetched by Makati Mayor Nemesio Yabut's helicopter. The one and only item on the agenda was the restoration of Antiporda, or how best to displace Arriola.

Manuel Molina, who was in the meeting, called Enrile's right-hand man, Alfonso Reyno, and told him about the meeting and the plan. Reyno informed Enrile, who in turn called a meeting of Cagayan mayors where he pressed for the ouster of Governor Dupaya. Reyno drafted a resolution for submission to the Cagayan Mayors League formalizing the governor's ouster.

★ ★ ★

The following day, Enrile went to Cagayan. At the Tuguegarao airport, he denounced the Dupayas before the press and the welcomers. The denunciation hit the headlines the following day. The President called Enrile by long distance telephone and told him to stop the attack on the Dupayas and to return to Manila at once.

Two days later, the President summoned Enrile, the Dupayas, and all the Cagayan mayors. Marcos asked Enrile to withdraw his stand against the Dupayas. Enrile declined. The mayors of Iguig and Amulong suggested to the President that a referendum be held in their towns for the people to decide.

The President called on Commission on Elections Chairman Leonardo Perez to conduct the referendum. This provoked a clamor for similar referenda throughout the country.

The next day, *Philippine Daily Express* columnist Teodoro F. Valencia phoned Enrile at home and asked for a meeting at the Manila Polo Club. Enrile agreed, and brought with him his personal physician, Dr. Emmanuel Almeda. Valencia was accompanied by Jess Sison.

Valencia suggested that Enrile forget the referendum proposal and settle the matter solely with the Dupayas. But Enrile stood his ground, and argued that what he was doing was good for the President. A few hours after the meeting, Local Governments Minister Jose Roño called Enrile at his office and said the First Lady wanted to talk to him. Enrile asked Roño to tell Mrs. Marcos that it would be pointless to talk to her if she would only ask him to compromise his position.

"But I will avoid a situation where I could be rude to her," he assured Roño.

Roño then suggested a luncheon meeting with the First Lady but Enrile begged off. Before noon, Roño was again on the phone, telling Enrile that the First Lady wanted to see him at the Technological Resources Center at 2 p.m. that day.

★ ★ ★

Enrile went there and was surprised at the "red carpet treatment." Kokoy was serving him coffee!

The League of Provincial Governors and Mayors was meeting at that time in the same place, purportedly to discuss implementation in the countryside of the government's tree planting program. In reality, it was a gathering to muster support for Governor Dupaya, who was present. Kokoy was chairman of the League.

The First Lady met Enrile in a private room but Enrile could sense that Governor Dupaya was inside an adjoining room and might be listening. Mrs. Marcos said Enrile should withdraw from his position. The answer was "no." Mrs. Marcos explained that the President needed the Dupayas in Cagayan.

"But how about the people of Cagayan, do they need her?" Enrile shot back, referring to Teresa, the governor.

Eventually, it was agreed that the President would ask Governor Dupaya to go on leave, and she did, spending her leave in the United States. The President then appointed Brig. Gen. Romeo Gatan, the PC regional command chief in the Cagayan Valley, as acting governor.

When she returned from the U.S. Governor Dupaya wanted to reassume her post. Enrile objected, but the President was for granting her request. It was Enrile's opinion that Governor Dupaya should not even run for reelection because she would lose and only embarass her backer, the President.

The President finally gave in to Enrile, and former Appellate Justice Justiniano Cortes, running unopposed, was elected in 1980.

★ ★ ★

A footnote with a romantic angle to this political episode needs to be told. Just before Governor Cortes took his oath of office, Enrile had Ver investigated secretly for possible involvement in the shooting and wounding of Ver's rival in the well-known *menage a trois* with his mistress. The rival, a businessman, was walking down the driveway of the Mandarin Hotel to board his Mercedes Benz when three armed men opened fire with their machine pistols. The businessman was hit in the left side of his face while his bodyguard, a nephew of Maj. Gen. Prospero A. Olivas, died trying to shield him with his body from a hail of bullets.

The victim, Boy Tuzon, was taken to the Makati Medical Center where he was placed under tight security by no other than the mistress, who had learned of the shooting from a friend. The security was so tight that even the businessman's wife was not allowed to visit him.

Two months later, the rival was again the target of gunmen. He had just attended a cockfight derby at Carangalan, Nueva Ecija, and was on his way home with a friend in his car when gunmen peppered the automobile with submachinegun bullets. He escaped unhurt but his companion died on the spot. The gunmen also exploded a handgrenade to complete the attack. He jumped out of the car unnoticed at the first volley, ran to a gasoline station and hid inside the men's room.

The gunmen escaped aboard a car which sped toward Manila. The rival later boarded a bus, and on reaching his house, called his parents. The next day, he and his parents were in the Office of Minister Enrile to tell him of the ambush.

With Enrile's help, the man left the country under an assumed name. He was accompanied by Col. Thelmo Cunanan, Enrile's chief of intelligence.

Meantime, the National Intelligence and Security Authority (NISA), headed by General Ver, had placed Enrile under close surveillance. Col. Igor Cepeda was assigned to supervise the operations.

When he learned of this, Enrile commented, "I could be the only defense minister in the entire world who is under surveillance by his own government."

★ ★ ★

On August 15, 1981, the President retired General Espino and appointed General Ver as his replacement. Three weeks later, Enrile was told that Ver had organized a hit team in Mindanao with orders to liquidate him. Enrile recruited some trusted men from the military and had them undergo training in anti-terror tactics under two retired instructors of the elite Special Air Service (SAS) Regiment of Great Britain. Galils and Uzis were also imported to arm the group.

On December 30, 1981, Alfie Anido, a young actor, was found dead in his room. The police ruled it a suicide. He died shortly after coming from a party with Enrile's daughter, Katrina. Ver's elite Presidential Security Command, showing unusual interest in the case, conducted its own investigation. Anido's death had occupied the headlines for days, and it was speculated that he was killed by Enrile's son, Jackie, after it was supposedly discovered that Anido had a quarrel with Katrina.

What the newspapers and magazines failed to report was that Anido had seen the President's daughter, Imee, dining with sportsman Tommy Manotoc at the Saigon Pearl restaurant in Makati the night before he was killed. It was the night Malacañang released a story that Tommy Manotoc, who was said to have secretly married Imee, had been kidnaped. As the kidnap story did the rounds of Manila's gossip centers, suspicion grew that the kidnaping had been stage-managed to abort an Imee-Tommy wedding. Now, if Anido had seen Manotoc that night at the restaurant and had lived to talk about it . . .

The Manotoc kidnapping was news for three weeks. Suddenly, out of the blue, Malacañang announced Manotoc's rescue from his captors following an alleged shootout with military agents under then Colonel Pedro Balbanero in the Sierra Madre mountains.

★ ★ ★

The rescue was played up in the newspapers and on television for days until Malacañang clamped a news blackout. Two months later, Manotoc and Imee publicly became husband and wife, and shortly after, parents of a boy, born in Hawaii.

Enrile's men resumed their training in Quezon province in July 1983. Marcos was furious when he got wind of it, and made no bones about it when he summoned Enrile and Fidel Ramos to the music room in Malacañang. The President confronted Enrile with the report. Enrile flatly denied it, and blamed it on intrigues from people he said were involved in shady deals and saw him as an obstacle in their illicit operations. As it turned out, the training was reported by a Colonel Visperas, who had been relieved from the Philippine Coconut Authority for anomalous disbursements of funds.

Enrile sensed that the President was dissatisfied with his explanation, so he said: "Why don't you allow me to leave if you don't trust me?"

General Ramos made the same request.

Marcos' reply was: "We have started this together; let's finish it together."

Enrile seized the chance to reach out: "Don't you realize you are a virtual prisoner here? The chief of staff controls the Presidential Security Command. His son, Irwin, is the PSU chief of staff. Another son, Rexor, is in charge of your close-in security, and Wyrlo is the armored unit chief.

"Balance your forces," Enrile and Ramos advised the President. "These people can put a manacle on you anytime and you would not be able to resist."

They could feel that the President was cool to their suggestion.

"He simply smiled," Enrile and Ramos recalled later.

Descending the stairs of the Palace on their way out, the two made a quick appraisal of the President. They concluded: "He is no longer the Marcos we know, the Marcos we idolize. He has changed a lot."

The seed was sprouting roots.

★   ★   ★

Enrile returned to his office and instructed his secretary to gather his papers and load them in his car. He also instructed an aide not to forget his diaries. He was going to make a careful study and analysis of the situation, and an accurate assessment would depend on the data recorded in those papers.

At home, he reflected on the First Lady's animosity towards him. Why had he been singled out for her wrath? He refused to accept as reasons the politics in Cagayan and his refusal to allow her friends to travel abroad. Only one avenue was left unexplored: the succession to the presidency. The thought brought to mind a report that the President had issued a secret decree on Jan. 14, 1975, naming the First Lady his successor in the event of his death or incapacitation.

The decree was for Mrs. Marcos to head a seven-man junta to be composed of the secretary of national defense, the secretary of finance, the secretary of trade, the secretary of local government, the secretary of foreign affairs, and the executive secretary.

The decree, numbered "100", was later amended by Presidential Decree 731, and issued in June of the same year, when the office of the Executive Secretary was abolished. The seat intended for the executive secretary went to the secretary of justice.

The decree was never made public although there was talk about its existence. It became public knowledge only when U.S. customs authorities found it among the documents seized from Mr. Marcos and his party when he fled to Hawaii on February 26, 1986.

★   ★   ★

In 1981, before leaving to attend the North-South Summit conference in Cancun, Mexico, Marcos instructed General Ver to implement the decree in the event of his death or incapacitation. A similar instruction was given to Ver when the President paid a state visit to Saudi Arabia with Mrs. Marcos. This particular instruction came with an additional taboo: Ver was to make sure that Enrile, who was the only Cabinet member not included in the official party, would not take over the government, whatever happened. The presidency after Marcos was reserved for only one person: the First Lady.

Enrile's thoughts went farther back. He recalled how on September 21, 1972, President Marcos placed the entire country under martial law "in order to save the republic and build a New Society." But two years later, something went wrong: the people were demoralized; the nation was practically a spiritual and moral wasteland; the democratic processes providing people a mechanism for change were inoperative, and the military was isolated from the people.

Enrile had suspected that early that the intention of martial law was not to give the republic a direction in development but to perpetuate the President in power.

The President had used the insurgency problem as a rationale for declaring martial law. At that time, there were only about 600 fully armed terrorists operating mostly in the Luzon area; members of the Central Committee of the Communist Party of the Philippines had almost all been captured.

But Enrile knew what he had to do. He kept his name clean, established a credibility of his own even as he rode along with the government to save his life and those of his family. Not to do so would have meant ending up six feet below or behind prison bars.

★ ★ ★

In 1978, Enrile recalled, the signs of hostility from the First Lady and General Ver, increased with unmistakable clarity: their feedback was that Enrile, with the backing of Ramos, had become a threat to the leadership of Marcos.

By 1982, barely four years later, the hostility became more pronounced. Civilian and military personnel in the government were brainwashed to shatter the myth of the popularity of Enrile and Ramos.

As their popularity grew, Marcos' health continued to deteriorate, Malacañang denials notwithstanding.

It was only logical for the First Lady and General Ver to firm up their plans to assume the mantle of leadership.

Enrile and Ramos knew this, and they were just as determined: Mrs. Marcos or General Ver should be stopped at all costs.

By that time, the core of the Enrile group which was to assist him and Ramos in preventing the Imelda Marcos-Ver takeover was ready. The training of soldiers in the Cagayan military command and the Reformist Movement was transferred from Quezon province to the Sierra Madre mountain ranges in the north, to avoid detection. But the secret was not safe from Ver. NISA beefed up its forces in Cagayan and monitored Enrile's movements, again on orders of the First Lady.

★ ★ ★

With Marcos' failing health becoming a guessing game — if he's okay today, will he be sick tomorrow? — it was not long before Enrile received a report indicating that the death of Marcos, would be kept secret for at least 72 hours to enable the First Lady and General Ver to consolidate the forces loyal and beholden to them.

Enrile's apprehensions over the tenacity of the First Lady and Ver in pursuing their plans for a takeover intensified when reliable sources within the Ver camp came up with revelation that the general had his own designs on the presidency!

According to the information, Ver would allow himself to be used at the start as a tool to facilitate the takeover by the First Lady upon Marcos' death or incapacitation. However, after a year or so, Ver would depose Mrs. Marcos and install himself as military dictator for life.

Ver composed his scheme by tightening his grip on power in the guise of promoting the presidential ambitions of Mrs. Marcos. In the process, he wrecked what little morale was left in the Armed Forces.

Ver tapped the NISA to implement his plan, which called for the penetration by military and police personnel of every town and city where he hoped to establish his political base. This was one of the reasons, as Enrile would recall later, why Ver had to place officers loyal to him in key positions not only in the Armed Forces but also in the national police. Significantly, in his speech on PC Day on August 1, 1983, President Marcos announced the transfer of operational control of the Integrated National Police from General Ramos to General Ver. Then, to prevent Enrile from possibly sabotaging Ver's grand plan for the AFP and the INP, the President beamed the message to Enrile by publicly describing Enrile as nothing more than his alter-ego.

The implications of Ver's political ambition on the armed forces and the INP were obvious. Until his ambition was realized, his key officers in the PC and INP would not be touched. Enrile's analysis: "This would mean also that the generals in the supporting cast who surrounded Ver could not be retired, to the prejudice of younger officers." One example was Army Chief Maj. General Fortunato Abat, a professional soldier, who was eased out in favor of his deputy, then Brig. Gen. Josephus Q. Ramas, a Marcos-Ver loyalist. Abat was exiled to China as Philippine ambassador.

As if the heavens rebelled at the thought of Ver succeeding, an unforeseen event all but put Ver in his place. The assassination of former Senator Benigno S. Aquino, Jr. on August 21, 1983 set back Ver's plans. Pressure was strong from all quarters on the President to remove him. Ver prepared an alternative plan for that eventuality. If he was relieved, Commodore Brillante Ochoco (the Coast Guard Chief) would be the chief of staff. Thus, Ver would remain in control with Ochoco at the helm, along with Ramas, Air Force Chief Maj. General Vicente Piccio, and their coterie.

The contingency plan also covered the possibility that General Ramos, not Ochoco, would be appointed chief of staff on Ver's retirement. As a fallback position, Ramos, who would still be surrounded by Ver loyalists, would be sent abroad as ambassador a few months after serving as chief of staff. In fact, President Marcos, once asked Enrile to suggest a suitable ambassadorial post for Ramos.

The Aquino assassination was to give Minister Enrile another reason to really fear for his life.

★ ★ ★

Normally, PC Day is celebrated on August 8, with the President as the traditional guest of honor and speaker. But in 1983, the celebration was advanced to August 1 because the President was gravely ill and has to undergo a kidney transplant on August 7. The operation was performed secretly at the Kidney Center in Quezon City.

Ver was not taking any chances. He moved 16 battalions to Metro Manila, ostensibly to join the PC Day parade. In truth, only three battalions joined the parade, the rest were deployed in and around the Palace and other areas in Metro Manila, neatly done to keep the soldiers away from the public. On August 14, a week after the operation, Enrile and other Cabinet members and some close friends of the Marcoses were called to Malacañang, but they had to wear sterilized gowns before they could see the President. "He was ambulant but still weak," Enrile recalled.

On August 21, 1983, a week after that visit, Aquino, a fraternity brother of the minister, was assassinated. Enrile was playing golf at the Alabang Country Club when he received a call from the President instructing him to proceed to the Army Station Hospital at Fort Bonifacio where Aquino's body had been taken. His assignment was to talk to the opposition leader's lawyers and relatives about the possibility of having the autopsy done right there in the hospital.

Enrile met with Aquino's mother and other relatives, and relayed to them the President's instructions.

When he saw the dead Aquino on the emergency table, Enrile was shocked: "My God, if they could do this to him, nobody is safe in this country anymore."

★ ★ ★

The day after Aquino's burial, a man, ostensibly from NISA, delivered to the Ministry of National Defense an intelligence report that Enrile was a target of assassination by New People's Army hit men from Concepcion, Tarlac, a crude way of insinuating that Aquino's followers suspected him of complicity in that assassination and were seeking out for blood.

The public clamored for a Warren Commission-type body to probe the assassination, and Marcos subsequently created a commission headed by then Chief Justice Enrique Fernando. Fernando's appointment drew such flak that the President was forced to drop him.

While he was looking for a replacement, the President called Enrile to Malacañang for advice on a possible replacement. Enrile mentioned Arturo Tolentino, but the President appeared cool to the suggestion.

When Enrile was about to leave the Palace, the President cautioned him: *Magingat ka sapagkat ikaw ay isa sa mga pinag-iinitan."* (Watch out because you're one of the targets.)

"It seemed the President knew of the NISA report," Enrile told his wife later.

Knowing that his life was in danger, he asked his wife to contact Fr. James Reuter, S.J., and to pass the word to Cardinal Sin.

The moves against Enrile continued without letup. The word was out. Enrile had made known his resistance to the Imelda Marcos-Ver takeover.

In the case of Ramos, the strategists of Mrs. Marcos and Ver must have cracked their skulls trying to figure a way to smear him. Unlike Enrile, who made controversial, if gutsy political moves, Ramos was non-controversial. He was just plain "Mr. Clean," a professional soldier doing a good job of it, which did not mean that Ramos was entirely free of Ver's machinations.

★ ★ ★

Even when Ver was on leave from the armed forces to stand trial for the murder of Ninoy Aquino, he could — and did — countermand the orders of the acting chief of staff, Fidel Ramos. Ramos had ordered the redeployment of 16 battalions to the countryside to check the rapid expansion of the NPA, but Ver and Imelda did not like it, and that was that. Only when Marcos had recovered from his kidney operation did Ramos bring up the matter again, and this time 10 battalions were sent back to the provinces. The remaining 6 battalions were placed under the operational control of the Presidential Security Command, where they remained up to the last day of the Marcos regime, February 25.

The break Imelda and Ver had been waiting for to make "Mr. Clean" look dirty came with the Escalante incident shortly before the snap presidential election.

On September 20, 1985, in Escalante town north of Bacolod City in Negros Occidental, constabulary and Civilian Home Defense Forces (CHDF) militiamen opened fire on a group of demonstrators. Nineteen civilians were killed.

There was public indignation. Ramos quietly and without much publicity dispatched a composite team of probers to Escalante to investigate and prosecute those involved in the carnage. Subsequently, Enrile created a fact-finding commision to undertake a similar probe.

The Enrile commission submitted its report, which the defense minister personally handcarried to Malacañang and submitted to the President. There was only one report, but Ver, with the collaboration of two friends in the media, made it appear that the Enrile commission had two separate reports, one by a majority of the members and another by a so-called minority. A press release planted in the newspapers alleged that the minority report recommended Ramos' indictment for administrative negligence on account of his alleged failure as constabulary and national police chief to conduct an immediate investigation of the massacre. Worse, the Ver-inspired press release also made it appear that Ramos had defended the PC and CHDF personnel involved in the massacre.

The truth was that, aside from there being no such thing as a separate minority report, the commission had cleared the Constabulary chief of any administrative or criminal liability.

★ ★ ★

Subsequent events tended to show that Marcos was part of the ploy to embarrass Ramos over the Escalante incident. The President used the spurious "minority report" as a convenient excuse to renege on his pre-election promise to retire General Ver. Every time mediamen pressed him to comment on Ver's overdue retirement and the appointment of his successor, the President would say he could not as yet accept Ver's resignation as chief of staff because a replacement had to be found, and General Ramos who was his logical successor could not be appointed because of his involvement in the Escalante incident.

Finally, on February 14, 1986, following a meeting with U.S. Ambassador Philip Habib, the President announced on TV that he was accepting Ver's retirement and that he was appointing Ramos chief of staff.

Ramos went to Malacañang the next day to check out the news, but he was told that Marcos had not signed any order to that effect.

"When Marcos announced Ver's resignation, I think he was just fooling us, fooling the entire world," Ramos later said.

In Cagayan, meanwhile, the Enrile forces activated their contingency plans, which by that time had shifted from securing Enrile's life and those of his family, to preventing Mrs. Marcos and General Ver from taking over in the event of Marcos' death.

★ ★ ★

Mid-1985, a segment of the officer corps identified with the Reform the Armed Forces Movement perceived Ver's tightening his stranglehold on the military to maximize Marcos' security. Military forces loyal to Ver were consolidating in Metro Manila. Extraordinary troop movements were taking place in and around the metropolis, involving particularly the Philippine Army under Maj. General Josephus Q. Ramas, a known devotee of the First Lady and General Ver.

The loyalists had a convenient cover for the unusual movement of manpower and hardware. It was disguised as a routine military exercise to ensure effective defense of the metropolis against possible terrorist attacks from the NPA. The cover was backed by propaganda.

Then came the surprise announcement on an American TV of the holding of a snap presidential election on February 7, 1986.

Up north in Enrile country, the elite "Cagayan 100," the hard core of the Reformist army, anticipated the events that would unfold days before and days after the election. The Cagayan military command, under Col. Tirso Gador, had a scenario complete with timetables. With the announcement of the February 7 polls, the covert plan was ready for execution. Link-ups were established between the province and the covert and overt command posts in the metropolis.

The "Cagayan 100," coincidentally, was to play an important role in the four-day revolution.

By the Comelec and Batasan counts, the opposition candidates — Corazon C. Aquino, widow of the assassinated senator, and former Senator Salvador H. Laurel — lost the election. But popular belief was that the opposition bets had won. Public indignation mounted; the revolutionary atmosphere intensified. But, lost in the euphoria of the Marcos-Tolentino victory, Marcos loyalists relaxed their guard. Even Mrs. Marcos and Ver appeared more tolerant of Enrile and Ramos.

But the Reformists did not allow themselves to be deceived by the seemingly relaxed atmosphere. They were waiting for Marcos to make his move to firm up his so-called victory, as widespread protest mounted over the fraudulent counting of votes and the summary proclamation of Marcos and his running mate, Member of Parliament Arturo M. Tolentino, by the Batasang Pambansa. The world's press was ganging up on him; Corazon Aquino was spearheading a snowballing campaign for civil disobedience. His back against the wall, Marcos had only one option open to him: Reimpose martial law.

Talk of martial law once more was in the air. The President denied it, but the more he denied it, the more the people believed it. Enrile, Ramos, and the Reformists, whose ranks had swelled, refused to be deceived.

Two days before the start of the Enrile-Ramos breakaway, the military force in Cagayan made a decision not to enforce martial law if it was reimposed. Instead, a plan was activated to undertake a pre-emptive move to prevent the reimposition of martial law and consequently the inauguration of President Marcos on February 25.

Possible dates for reimposition of martial law, according to the scenario, were February 22 and February 23, or at most 72 hours before the inauguration. Colonel Gador estimated that the gathering of friendly forces to prevent the procalamation of martial law and the swearing in of Marcos would have to be completed 48 to 72 hours before those dates.

February 22 and 23, the crucial dates, fell on a weekend. People, including the military, would be taking it easy. A rest period. A break. Even for the troops. Perfect for the loyalists: the right time to impose martial rule.

Going by his calendar, Gador fixed the 72 hours before the oath-taking on February 25 falling on Saturday, the 22nd of February — exactly two weeks after the elections.

It was time to press the button on the "Cagayan 100" for their rendezvous with history.

Troops under Colonel Gador were deployed in three waves towards the Sierra Madre supposedly for a massive offensive against the New People's Army.

In the evening of February 19, the first wave left PC headquarters in full combat gear aboard a military truck which took them to Peñablanca, where they quartered in the barracks until shortly before daylight. They were ordered to change to civilian clothes and to board a chartered bus. But they were to leave behind their gear, including their firearms, all properly tagged.

They boarded the bus at 5 in the morning of February 20 and debarked at the Quezon Memorial Circle in Quezon City where they were told to await further orders. Up to that point, the men had not been told of their mission.

★ ★ ★

February 21, Enrile's Fokker plane, *Cristina*, left Villamor Air Base for Cagayan. Its mission: to collect the soldiers' combat gear, including firearms, and bring them to Villamor Air Base.

Colonel Gador, by this time already in Camp Aguinaldo, was in touch with his officers in Cagayan.

Using a pre-arranged code, Gador was being informed by telephone, thus:

"Sir, the tabletops have been loaded for delivery. The chairs will follow as soon as the loading vehicles arrive."

The tabletops were soldiers; the chairs were firearms.

Lunchtime, February 21, the *Cristina* left Villamor Air Base to pick up the firearms at the Tuguegarao airport. At 3 p.m. of the same day, it was back at Villamor Air Base. The firearms were to be kept inside the plane at the *Cristina's* hangar until the following day.

February 22, two other waves of troops arrived in Quezon City from Cagayan.

They were transported to Camp Aguinaldo and billeted just behind the defense ministry.

At 4:30 in the afternoon, Enrile requested for helicopters to fly the *Cristina* cargo to Camp Aguinaldo.

Minutes later, the helicopters arrived and their cargo unloaded for distribution to the troops. Only then was the Cagayan force told of their mission: to neutralize the Military Police Brigade in Camp Aguinaldo and to secure the perimeter of the defense ministry building.

The tension peaked.

★   ★   ★

At 6 p.m., the telephone at the Social Hall of the Ministry of National Defense building rang. General Ver was on the other end of the line. Enrile spoke, listened, talked, listened. Then finally he told General Ver:

"The die is cast. We have already broken the shell of the egg. The only thing left to do is to stir it . . ." □

CHAPTER VI

"For it is certain that the less a man is acquainted with the sweets of life, the less reason he has to be afraid of death."

— Vegetius

THE RISE OF PEOPLE POWER

The events that set the stage for the four-day revolution took years to pile up into a mass abomination.

Even prior to the August 21 assassination of former Senator Benigno S. Aquino, Jr., and the capital flight it set off, Philippine business and industry had come to a slow wilt. The cost of running plants and mills, maintaining buildings and offices and sustaining an increasingly plaintive manpower had skyrocketed.

Faced with a four-fold increase in prices of oil and petroleum products, the merchants and industrialists alike were confronted with a singular, if bitter, option: cut back on the workforce so that money saved on salaries and wages could pay for raw materials and power bills.

This was to be the cycle through the late seventies and toward the eighties, as it made a turn for the worst recession the economy was ever to be inflicted with. More than half a million people were thrown out of jobs.

Propped up by massive loans and aid from abroad, the Marcos administration retaliated, to no avail, with numerous infrastructure projects. Billions of pesos that were poured into the construction of roads, bridges, schools, ports, and parks failed to absorb the unemployed.

By 1984, widespread joblessness had begun to swell the ranks of protesters in urban centers.

The "parliament of the street," as mammoth rallies would be called in Metro Manila, burst upon the political scene literally howling for radical changes in the nation's business life. With inflation raging at 40 per cent, even those with jobs could hardly make both ends meet. On the other hand, harassed with high interest rates on credit from banks, employers found themselves utterly helpless to bring relief to the labor sector.

Employee and employer would soon enough find themselves confronting each other in the picket lines on an average of one strike a day between 1984 and 1985.

Where labor and management shared a perception of common plight — an economy distorted by crony capitalism and massive graft in high places — they found themselves linking arms in protest rallies against the government.

To this upsurge of discontent, the Marcos regime responded in the worst political terms. Demonstrators were dealt with brutally, their leaders persecuted or hunted down.

Businessmen, in sympathy with the protesters, found themselves discriminated against and sometimes even totally blocked from deals with the government.

The media, which were expected to mirror national developments, were placed in blinkers — prompting independent journalists to set up "the alternative press." Denied free access to government information, the rebel sector of media turned for their sources to an increasingly radicalized business-labor-academic bloc.

The first match was struck in the long night of confrontation with the Marcos clique. The government itself, probably under pressure from abroad, would help pave the way to the four-day showdown on that now historic strip of Epifanio delos Santos Avenue.

Heavily criticized and losing his popularity as well as his credibility, Marcos grudgingly agreed to the holding of the February 7 special Presidential and Vice-Presidential polls. Men around the President balked at the prospect of having to face an impoverished and disenchanted electorate. Regardless, the elections were set. Uncle Sam was watching.

Foreign lenders, led by the International Monetary Fund and the

World Bank to whom the country owed some $26 billion, demanded assurance that their loans would be honored.

What better guarantee of this than for the government, Marcos in particular, to be elected or given a new mandate to manage the political and economic affairs of the country?

The country's major trading partners, who for obvious reasons were most keenly interested in having the loans released, were all for holding the election.

Thus, the extraordinary concern shown by both the United States and Japan "for the honest, clean and free" exercise of suffrage by 23 million Filipinos.

And so to the polls.

The Marcos government felt invincible. In the last 20 years it had set in place the most formidable political machinery ever to hold sway over the country: a command network reaching out from Malacañang to the remotest province, town and barangay.

Via its Masagana 99 program, the government had channeled billions into the countryside, placing in its debt hundreds of thousands of miracle rice farmers totally dependent on state-produced or imported fertilizers.

The administration's grip strangled the vast coconut and sugar plantations; likewise it placed the mining industry under its heel with huge loans from state banks.

With enormous sums accumulated from people's contributions to the Social Security System and the Goverment Service Insurance System, the government had more than 50 per cent of its assets in the banking and finance system.

This was not to mention crony capitalist hoards from which the Marcos clique would draw billions to finance the campaign.

Finally, it had the National Treasury for emergency advances and the Central Bank to print, if need be, all the election pesos for the usual vote-buying.

The polls were nothing less than a cinch.

The opposition had hardly anything going for it. Weeks away from the February 7 polls, it continued to be leaderless, fragmented, and short of logistics.

When it finally found a rallying point in the person of Corazon C. Aquino, widow of the slain Benigno S. Aquino, Jr., courtesy of the Catholic Church's irrepressible Jaime Cardinal Sin, the opposition wanted, as much as it needed, a source of real inspiration.

It had neither ideology nor a program of government to offer to the electorate. Under normal conditions and in normal climes, the Aquino-led opposition would have been a very sad political contrivance.

But the times were far from normal. The loam of popular grievances against the Marcos regime was there, waiting to be cultivated, so soft it was going to yield and be turned up by the crudest political hoe.

The Gross National Product, by which the sum total of employment and production was measured, had slid down by more than five per cent, or roughly ₱10 billion based on GNP ₱200 billion.

Of the one million out of work, about half of the 18-million-strong labor force were under-employed or seeking additional income. Illiterate households in the countryside kept sending unemployables to the cities, thousands to Manila's squatter colonies and congested districts. The campuses, too, were generously contributing to the ranks of the jobless. On the side of the business and industrial communities, tight money and credit caused retrenchments and mass layoffs. More than 30 per cent of the top 1,000 corporations suffered serious setbacks, posting bottom lines in red for the first time. Even flagship firms, like San Miguel Corporation and Ayala Corporation, had to drop hundreds from their personnel rosters. Towards the end of 1985, more than 300 medium-sized companies were reported by the Securities and Exchange Commission to have sought permission to bow out of business.

The economy was in shambles, in sharp contrast to the wealth that the Marcos regime was ready to draw on to fund a new mandate.

Mass poverty and the 20-year long powerlessness of the people under Marcos' authoritarian rule became the main issues of the February 7 elections.

The Corazon C. Aquino-Salvador H. Laurel tandem raised the issues of unemployment, high prices, and violation of human and civil rights against the government.

The Ferdinand E. Marcos-Arturo M. Tolentino team ran on a national recovery platform and an anti-communist stance.

Four days into the counting of votes cast on February 7, the Aquino camp came into a disastrous one-and-a-half million drubbing in the "official" Commission on Elections tally.

The following week, amidst public uproar against the fraudulent conduct of the elections, the Batasang Pambansa proclaimed Marcos' reelection for a new six-year term.

Aquino gathered more than a million people at the Luneta to show she had in fact won but had been robbed of victory. She called for national civil disobedience to dramatize the nation's mass abhorrence for the theft of an election.

By then, Aquino had emerged as a political phenomenon in the country, a magnet attracting millions of bitterly disaffected Filipinos.

Yet, her defeat at Marcos' hands would momentarily catapult her to the role of symbol of mass indignation against a seemingly invincible regime.

Aquino was island-hopping in Southern Philippines, as the "Joan of Arc" of civil disobedience, when the fateful decision was made by Defense Minister Juan Ponce Enrile and Lt. Gen. Fidel V. Ramos, the

AFP vice chief of staff, to break away from Marcos' government.

On February 22, barely 15 days after the fraudulent polls that ushered in the Aquino civil disobedience drive, the civilian and military heads of the Marcos government breached the limit of allegiance to the Commander-in-Chief.

A call to higher defiance had been sounded.

The millions who marched behind the *Laban* sign only to be crushed at the polls by the Marcos juggernaut would discover in a flash a new and more dangerous cause: Enrile and Ramos raising the banner of people-oriented reforms in the Armed Forces of the Philippines, the reestablishment of loyalty to the Constitution, the state, and to no man.

Initially, only a few hundred officers and soldiers were reported to have joined up with Enrile and Ramos at Camp Aguinaldo. The full strength of the Reform Movement in the military was yet to reveal itself. Apparently, therefore, it was totally up to the people of Manila and environs to uphold the cause of Enrile and Ramos against the deadly forces of Malacañang.

So, when the signal to keep the light on in Camp Aguinaldo by way of a people's vigil was given by Cardinal Sin using Radio Veritas' broadcast facilities, men and women from all walks of life trooped to Epifanio delos Santos Avenue (EDSA).

Why would hundreds and, in just a matter of hours, hundreds of thousands risk their all at EDSA to shield Marcos' wayward duo? The question may well engage psychologists and sociologists for years to come.

However, conditions in the years prior which continued to prevail up to that point on EDSA, and indeed up to the present, suggested a preparedness which history could not have avoided even if it wanted to. The Filipino masses had been through an economic and political wringer under two decades of Marcos rule and discontent had so engulfed their minds and hearts that those who turned communist or communist sympathizers were thought to have done the right thing.

Others, among them the nation's finest professionals, had gone abroad in search for opportunities they felt could no longer be found in their country.

But for the many who would not buy the Marxist solution or who could not migrate, only one option was left: to recast existing social, economic and political institutions along more bearable, if not immediately acceptable, lines.

It is on this middle road that the majority of Filipinos found themselves as partisans, either of Aquino or Marcos. Divided into two major camps, they would be united in their desire for change, though divided in their choice of leader. It was a common search for change in the status quo, though the searching would be done under separate party banners. The shared frustrations that followed the hopeful partisanship of the February 7 polls, polarized the nation, bringing it to the brink of a civil war.

Established churches, notably the Roman Catholic church, constantly urged the faithful to rely on the power of prayer against inequity. Prayers soothed the people's hurt for a while. But as speculations on the re-imposition of martial law heightened, fear and anger began to well up again. Understandably, the Aquino partisans, especially the professionals, businessmen and industrialists, were the most agitated.

The workers, peasants and the jobless were impatient but largely at a loss about what precisely was to be done about the worsening political, economic and social conditions.

It was precisely this moment, perhaps it was in the nick of time, that the Enrile-Ramos break from the Marcos government took place. It caught the tide of elite agitation and mass impatience.

The phenomenon at EDSA illustrated the instant melt-down of partisan divisions for a total blending of people into "people power," a force assuredly political and unabashedly righteous. The fact that people power was also prayerful, with nuns, priests and ministers leading the supplicant crowd in canticles and chants did not preclude its willingness to be harnessed to resist violence.

For, where the Aquino leadership could but be fierce in its advocacy of change, the Enrile-Ramos leadership was that, too, and more so because it had the capacity for ferocity. Hindsight now indicates that where the masses behind the Aquino crusade would have felt helpless before Marcos' armed partisans, the same masses would not have felt so defenseless because of the military quality of the Enrile-Ramos reform movement.

In a word, people and soldiers had found themselves at last. Shared economic sufferings, which made allegiance to the accountable regime untenable, built the bridge between them.

Sympathy from the media and their audiences abroad also assumed a key role in the molding of the people power that installed Aquino as the first woman Head of State in the Philippines. When Marcos needed the exposure least, internationally circulated American magazines, notably *Newsweek* and *Time*, periodically came out with cover stories on the Philippine situation. Media coverage in the United States was extended to the activities and statements of Filipino leaders in exile, which gave the Marcos propaganda machine the herculean task of rebutting and being believed.

Closer to Manila, newspapers and magazines based in Tokyo and Hongkong also did an admirable job of reporting and commenting on the local scene. In Europe, especially in London where a sizable colony of Filipinos resides, sharply critical articles on the lifestyle of the ruling family and their friends appeared in major publications.

As all these filtered into the country through clippings, letters and photocopies smuggled in by returning travellers, locals at the forefront of the anti-Marcos campaign began to feel less and less alone. The knowledge that the struggle to unshackle the country was becoming a global concern emboldened more and more of the so-called silent majority to make uncomfortable noises for Marcos.

Manila's coffeeshops, where middle class intellectuals and political outsiders regularly congregate with media people and business executives, served not just rivers of coffee by mile-long reports on what the rest of the world had been saying about the country. Habitues would pass on the media morsels to family and neighbors to set off a community-to-community relay that in time far outstripped the reach of local newspapers friendly or even subservient to the Marcos regime.

In Makati's Ayala district, for instance, a Xeroxed anti-Marcos article published in a foreign publication became coveted reading fare no matter how old or outdated it had become.

The constant exchange of information in the coffeeshops, replicated aboard jeepneys and buses and at corner stores, brought spirits critical of the regime closer, nudging them nearer the point of convergence that would rise as people power at EDSA.

Foreign opinion would land with full impact on the minds of the populace, especially when it began descending from the US Congress, the Japanese Diet and, later, from the halls of the Australian Parliament.

If the world cared, why shouldn't Filipinos?

So it was, that when official and unofficial fact-finding missions arrived from the US, Japan, Australia, Britain, and the World Court and Amnesty International, willing informers from major segments of Philippine society were easy to locate.

Trade and business chambers contributed insights on the nation's troubled economy. Civic and political groups "advertised" how the government handled national affairs. The Roman Catholic Church, Cardinal Sin, in particular, was every foreign fact-finding mission's favorite source of intelligence.

Most of the missions left with a rich catch of documentation on torture, liquidation, illegal arrest, large-scale corruption, scandalous extravagance amid cruel poverty.

But if the world were being told of the Filipinos' misfortune, what were they doing about it? The peasants of Central Luzon, north of Manila, have organized themselves into provincial associations, later into a regionwide federation pressing for a more vigorous and equitable implementation of agrarian reform. The migrant workers of sugar plantations in Western Visayas, on the island of Negros in particular, organized themselves with the help of Catholic and Protestant missionaries. Labor unions, notably the radical *Kilusang Mayo Uno* (May 1st Movement), agitated for broader workers' rights and more effective protection for laborers wishing to unionize. Politicalization of the peasant, labor and youth organization was stepped up by intellectuals from universities and business communities. Social work by the religious sectors took on the added burden of opening the eyes of countryside residents to the rights the Marcos regime said it would respect but did not.

Though in ways as divergent as their callings, countless men and women embarked on a mission to vindicate their honor and freedom as a people. Individuals or groups, they had a singular goal: the dismantling of the Marcos network of corruption, repression and irresponsibility.

The campaign to dislodge Marcos or, at the very least to compel him to accommodate popular clamor for change, had been going on for a long time before it was to realize its full potency as a countervailing force. In street confrontations, violent dispersals on Mendiola street leading to Malacañang and along Manila's major thoroughfares time and again proved the protesters' initial vulnerability. But they would learn soon enough to adjust to their frailty, and collect themselves into bigger, stronger protest groups.

Against this background of popular protest, Aquino's reluctant presidential aspiration became a determined presidential candidacy.

The opposition's National Unification Council and Convenors Group encouraged by Cardinal Sin, had done its job picking the person to pit against Marcos. The parliament of the streets reverberated with the call to rally behind the widow of the assassinated senator, and millions responded.

In Manila and all over the country, the Aquino-Laurel ticket running under the banner of the United Nationalist Democratic Organization would draw record crowds. Partisans over fifty would recall that even the charismatic Ramon Magsaysay, defense minister of the Quirino years, had not gathered such huge throngs although he would be elected President by an unprecedented landslide.

The Aquino campaign gave mass action the muscle required for the olympian exertion it was destined to demand at EDSA in a few months.

With the Marcos administration compelled to allow longer leash to political activity over most of the country, even the more loosely organized antiregime factions were able to interact with purposive counterparts. In cities and provinces, in the guise of constitutional enterprise, partisan caucuses, strategy meetings and campaign planning sessions were held by diverse groups, including those with a marked ideological slant. The military establishment, previously inclined to view mass assemblies with reflexive suspicion, for the first time in years played the game of maximum tolerance.

The permissiveness fostered by the February 7 polls made room for "freedom at midnight" which, to the eternal envy of a Gandhian convert, would break into daylight and prevail over the Marcos darkness, bloodlessly, in a wink of history. God, the author of circumstance, would momentarily place the rise of people power in check with the controversial triumph of Marcos at the polls and shunt Aquino's crusade to the political sidelines. Then, in one mystical flash of human inspiration, two men who were with Marcos when he established the foundations of a purportedly reformist and transitional iron rule, crashed through the wall of official hyprocrisy.

February 22, as noontime ebbed, Enrile and Ramos holed up separately in Camp Aguinaldo and Camp Crame, decided to await fate and the people's verdict. Overnight, the same masses who had but lately thronged Aquino's campaign rallies set up an impenetrable human wall around Camp Crame in anticipation of an assault by Marcos forces.

The magic of the electronic media would bring the mighty spectacle of millions of unarmed yet undaunted Filipinos overwhelming Marcos' tank battalions with prayers, flowers, food, smiles — with peace. Prometheus Unbound became incarnate in the Filipino and the rise of people power hit zenith before the eyes of the world. It has since been a difficult tale to tell for all its truth and, perhaps, precisely because of its utmost veracity. ☐

CHAPTER VII

It is our basic aim to establish a unique martial tradition for the nation which envisages that in the event we are compelled to intervene in the political life of the nation in order to save it, the Members pledge to each other, that they shall not exercise political power, and that they shall return to their barracks as soon as the sovereign will of the people has prevailed.

— RAM Manifesto, 1986

THE RAM

Toward A Unique Martial Tradition

When Defense Minister Juan Ponce Enrile and Armed Forces Vice Chief of Staff Lt. Gen. Fidel V. Ramos flung the gauntlet at the Marcos monolith, they were not as vulnerable or as helpless as the nation and the world might have thought them to be.

The people were clearly in a revolutionary mood. Almost daily, citizens by the hundreds of thousands were pouring into the streets to protest not only the subverting of their will at the presidential polls, but also the two decades of repression and oppression under the Marcos autocracy.

Mrs. Corazon Aquino, who was robbed of the presidency by the Marcos-controlled Commission on Elections and the Batasang Pambansa (parliament) which declared Marcos winner based on spurious election returns, was spearheading a massive civil disobedience campaign and had called for a nationwide boycott of crony corporations and other business establishments that had supported the Marcos regime.

So successful was the boycott that many sectors of the business community whose products and services became targets crumbled under the weight of the popular movement.

So when Enrile and Ramos burst upon the scene, they had the people clearly behind them. But they could not have imagined using the people's support as a weapon against the Marcos juggernaut, much less bank on it. They knew the people had only their indignation and hatred of Marcos to fight him with; the weapons of death that win wars and crush revolts were with the Marcos military.

Enrile and Ramos had something else in mind: the Reform the Armed Forces Movement (RAM) both in the officer corps and the rank and file, whose membership had swelled to more than 4,000 since it was organized on July 23, 1982 by five young officers led by Col. Gregorio Honasan.

The organization of the RAM was a reaction of the young and idealistic officers to the widespread corruption in the ranks, favoritism in farming out promotions, babying of long retireable generals which stunted their own career, rampant abuses against civilians, discrimination in the allocation of supplies, and the use of military units and paramilitary units to thwart the national will at the polls during elections.

To spread the gospel of reforms not only in the officer corps but also in the rank and file, "Gringo" Honasan, as he was called, and the four other founding members organized other groups which, in turn, inspired the organization of others until a nationwide ripple effect was achieved.

Honasan and his group traveled to the provinces and dialogued with any number of their comrades-in-arms who cared to listen. They came back each time with glowing reports of how they were received with more than just idle curiosity, by junior officers especially, indicating the success of the movement.

The task, nevertheless, was formidable. The men in uniform, especially those in the field, were engrossed in the grim business of fighting the enemies of the state. Their training compels them to obey orders first and complain later, it is difficult to make them understand the nation they were defending with their lives was moving to an undesirable direction, and that they were being used to promote personal rather than national interest.

A serious search for leaders of the small group was launched from among the more senior, only to find out from them a common reticence to lead. They were either too high to be non-partisan (owing their positions to the powers that be), too comfortable to be interested, or too wealthy to care.

Their open frankness was admirable, the young officers thought, for they have, in their own way, admitted that they no longer have the moral right to lead the reform movement.

The conventional fora to ventilate their grievances and aspirations were out of the question, too. They had already been denied this venue mainly because of the prevailing military culture that was evolved in the 1980s — rewarding the boot-licking incompetents and banishing independent-minded professionals and achievers.

Then came the shot that snuffed the life of a returning hero at the Manila International Airport tarmac on August 21, 1983. Heard around the world, the shot that felled Benigno S. Aquino, Jr. shocked and pricked the conscience of the Filipino nation, and awakened the armed forces.

In one of their meetings, an 11-man steering committee, which had by this time been organized to put a direction to the organization made an analysis of the Aquino assassination and they came up with this conclusion: "Aquino could not have been assassinated by a lone gunman without the go-signal by some people from the highest chain of command, considering that the airport was fully secured by more than 1,000 highly-trained men where infiltration was impossible!"

The Reformists shared the feeling of Minister of Defense Juan Ponce Enrile who exclaimed on seeing the body of the fallen hero: "Nobody is safe in this country anymore!"

They moved fast, recouped and institutionalized the virtues of discipline, honor, honesty, and service to the country. They pledged not to use violence to achieve their objective, nor abet any kind of coup. They used reason and persuasion, and the moral force of good in fighting for reforms within the chain of command and within the framework of the grievance mechanism in the code of conduct.

But they would fight — with force and at the sacrifice of their lives if necessary — any attempt to rob the people further of their democratic heritage. They could no longer stomach what was happening. They could no longer remain hapless witnesses to the degeneration of the military — and the nation.

Thus on March 21, 1985 at the Philippine Military Academy alumni homecoming day in Baguio City, which coincided with the Academy's graduation exercises for Class '85, some 300 members of the RAM demonstrated in front of the graduating class and guests, including President Marcos, who was the traditional keynote speaker at the commencement rites. The Reformists sported T-shirts with the legend "We belong . . ." (short for the group's name — "We Belong to the Reform the AFP Movement"), and waved banners and carried placards demanding reform in the military organization.

Marcos quickly dismissed the group's demand for reforms as mere "griping."

"Griping in the Armed Forces is traditional, but they just called it by an esoteric name," the President said. He did not realize that it was already the opening salvo in the uprising that was to end his regime.

At 10 a.m. on Saturday, February 22, Gringo Honasan was in his office behind the Defense Ministry building, checking out incoming reports for additional data on the prepositioning of troops and armored vehicles in Malacañang and other places in Metro Manila where vital installations are located. As he pored over some of the documents on the table, two brief reports which came in at 7 a.m. caught his eye: "5th Marine Battalion Landing Team moved to Pandacan area just off the Otis entrance of the Malacañang Park from Fort Bonifacio at 0400H" (4 a.m.).

"14th Army Infantry Battalion moved to North Harbor from Nueva Ecija at 0300H" (3 a.m.)

Gringo asked his intelligence officer, Lt. Col. Eduardo "Red" Kapunan, to report to his office at once. "Metro Manila is surrounded with troops!" Honasan informed Red Kapunan.

"This is it, man!" Red said. Gringo, lifted the hotline to the minister. It was dead. He tried another telephone. It was dead, too. "Let's go to the minister." Gringo said, hoping Enrile had not been arrested yet.

As they were leaving, Col. Rolando Abadilla, intelligence chief of the Philippine Constabulary's Metropolitan Command, arrived. He had a message. "Greg, General Ver is asking you not to attack Malacañang, after all you and Irwin (Ver's son, who is a colonel) are good friends and your father and the general also are good friends . . ."

"We have no such intention," Honasan assured Abadilla.

The subject was dropped. The two walked out casually. Abadilla nodded and said, "See you later."

Honasan and Kapunan skipped the usual route to the minister's residence, 13 kilometers south of Camp Aguinaldo and maintained radio silence. As they drove into the entrance, they saw the minister's car. "He's all right." Gringo told Red.

After his meeting with Enrile, during which they discussed alternative plans to meet the emergency, Gringo picked up his radio transceiver and barked orders to his radio operator at Camp Aguinaldo: "Joggers, Joggers!" It was the signal to put all his men and RAM people, including the 300 civilian components, on combat readiness.

At Camp Aguinaldo, 12 teams, each with four men were immediately organized from the civilian components. Their job was to contact all RAM members in the 12 Regional Unified Commands (RUC) of the Armed Forces with the fastest means of communication, using coded signals.

Within two hours the Philippine Long Distance Telephone Company was flooded with requests for connections from different places in Metro Manila, including hotels where civilian Reformists had checked in for the purpose. By 4 p.m., the job was completed.

There was another assignment: Conduct surveillance and undertake evacuation operations for RAM families in Metro Manila.

Navy Capt. Proceso Maligalig, Naval Operations assistant chief, was in his office at 4:30 that afternoon when he received a call from Lt. (jg) Alex Pama of the defense ministry. "Sir, our tennis game is postponed until tomorrow. Okay?"

"Okay!" Maligalig yelled and dropped the phone.

"Postponed" was the key word, the signal to activate "Operation Twiggy," the contingency plan for the Reformists in the Navy. Maligalig called Navy Capt. Carlito Cunanan, Naval Operating Forces deputy chief, in his quarters at Sangley Point, Cavite. He was not there. Neither was his wife.

It was in Cubao, Quezon City, where Cunanan and his wife were visiting with a friend that Captain Cunanan received a call from his younger brother, Army Col. Thelmo Cunanan, Minister Enrile's intelligence officer. He was told to watch TV and listen to Radio Veritas at 6:30 p.m.

While waiting for the telecast, Carlito telephoned Navy Capt. Carlos Agustin at the office of Ambassador Benjamin "Kokoy" Romualdez at Aguado, across Malacañang Palace. He told Agustin of his brother Thelmo's desire that they work for the Enrile-Ramos camp. Agustin, the defense attache in Washington, was in Manila and had helped coordinate the activities of American officials who had been in town to observe the elections.

Agustin agreed. He and Lt. Commander Normando D. Naval, another Reformist in the Navy, immediately organized an intelligence task force together with retired Navy Capts. Victor L. Mamon and Buenaventura B. Desquitado, and Lt. (jg) Renan Suarez. They contacted their friends and classmates in the military, including Col. Plaridel M. Abaya, RUC 3 deputy chief. Abaya had a heartening sidebar report on how the Reformists neutralized the 5th Army Division and the RUC 3 command, preventing it from sending reinforcements to the loyalist camp of President Ferdinand Marcos and his Armed Forces chief of staff, General Fabian C. Ver.

The task force made periodic assessments of the situation, which they distributed to friends in the US defense attache's office and the CIA station, headed by Norbert Garett. The reports carefully detailed the snowballing support the Enrile-Ramos cause was generating from the AFP officer corps as well as from the rank and file. Buttressed by actual accounts of the defections which were slowly but surely sapping the strength of the Marcos-Ver war machine, these assessments no doubt contributed to the strengthening of the US government's resolve to "persuade" Marcos to leave the country.

One of those who prepared the reports and assessments, Maj. Vic Raphael of the US Defense attache's office, was in constant touch with his good friends, Honasan, Kapunan, and other Reformist officers. Carlito returned to the base and proceeded directly to his quarters. A few minutes later, Maligalig was on the phone telling him about Pama's call. Carlito said he knew about it and instructed him to monitor movements of ships and troops identified with the Marcos-Ver clique.

When Minister Enrile moved to Camp Crame to join General Ramos, Col. Antonio Samonte and Navy Capt. Warlino Sadiarin, both Reformist officers holding key positions in the Armed Forces Intelligence Service, remained at ISAFP headquarters in Camp Aguinaldo from where they carefully monitored the activities of loyalist forces through their agents. Their reports provided the Enrile-Ramos camp with accurate assessments of the situation in Fort Bonifacio, Malacañang Park and the regional commands.

Carlito made a few more calls after instructing his men at the Naval Operating Forces headquarters to go on full red alert and be ready to join Minister Enrile. Then he called Commodore Tagumpay Jardiniano, his chief, to tell him that he was joining the minister and that some officers in his command had already defected. Jardiniano told Carlito he was joining them, too, but asked that it be kept a secret in the meantime for security reasons.

Carlito relayed the good news to Minister Enrile through his younger brother. "Good!" the minister said, and passed it on to General Ramos.

Rear Admiral Brillante Ochoco, Navy flag officer in command, was unaware of what was going on in his command. He was in Malacañang most of the time, and only after midnight of Sunday did he know that 85 per cent of the Navy was already on the Enrile-Ramos side. By Monday morning, shortly before dawn, two Navy ships were at the mouth of the Pasig River, their guns pointed at the Palace. Two other ships, anchored off the Rizal Park, had their guns also directed at the Malacañang Park, which is adjacent to the headquarters of the Presidential Security Command. By this time, General Ramos had announced the defection of the entire Navy command, with the exception of Commodore Ochoco and a few loyal followers.

At the War Room in Camp Crame, Enrile and Ramos wondered why the Air Force had not yet responded to their call for support. Honasan and Lt. Col. Tito Legaspi had the good news.

"We have talked to the Air Force people, and they are just waiting for the right time to fly their choppers to us," they told the minister. They also reported that Col. Antonio F. Sotelo, the 15th Strike Wing commander, had assured Col. Hector Tarrazona he would be joining along with Maj. Charles Hotchkiss, commander of the 20th Squadron of the 15th Strike Wing.

"How about the fighter pilots at Basa Air Base?" Ramos asked.

"They are with us, Sir!" Legaspi replied. He said Maj. Francisco P. Baula, Jr., the squadron commander of the 5th Fighter Wing would be coming in with two of his pilots, Ist Lts. Nestor A. Genuino, Jr. and Noe P. Linsangan.

After their meeting with Enrile and Ramos, the two officers conferred with Colonel Kapunan in another room. They asked Kapunan to activate contingency plans for Villamor Air Base and Basa Air Base, in case the pilots had a last-minute change of heart.

The contingency operations, which they had rehearsed for weeks, called for the capture of the two bases with the use of 12 commando teams from the PC Special Action Force under Lt. Col. Rey Velasco and Colonel Kapunan. The commando teams, each with four men, would sneak into the camps simultaneously with the aid of Reformist officers inside and seize all the helicopters and jet fighters, to be flown outside the bases by RAM pilots. The perimeters of the two bases would then be secured by two companies from the PC Training Command under Col. Bayani Fabic.

Twelve other teams from Honasan's and Kapunan's groups under Maj. Arsenio Santos and Lt. Andy Gauran would launch diversionary operations nearby, blowing up gasoline tanks, buildings and hangars.

One of the RAM officers involved in the planning was Lt. Col. Rey Rivera. In the evening of February 21, Rivera received a call from Honasan who told him that martial law might be declared within the next 48 or 72 hours. He was also informed that arrest orders for RAM members had been signed by the President.

Rivera was scheduled to leave the next day for the United States to undergo schooling on comptrollership at Sheppard Air Force Base in Texas. Honasan called to tell Rivera to proceed with his trip and leave the concerns of the Movement to the rest of the guys.

"We prepared for this a long time and you're telling me to go? No way!" Rivera barked his defiance.

Honasan was insistent, but Rivera was equally determined not to go. To abort his trip, Rivera had his right foot cast in plaster to make it look like he had sprained an ankle during a tennis match.

He personally reported to Col. Vicente Buenaventura, his immediate superior at the defense ministry comptroller's office, and suggested that, because of this condition, his alternate, Commander Ubaldo Villafuerte, be sent in his place.

At 6:30 p.m., while Enrile and Ramos were announcing their breakaway from Marcos, Rivera was with Kapunan, Maj. Renato Ramos, Capt. Pompeo Limbo, Capt. Roberto Damian and Lt. Marcelino Mendoza in the ministry's conference room planning an escape route for Enrile, in case Camp Aguinaldo was attacked. They assumed that Malacañang would employ a minimum of two battalions from the Presidential Security Command (PSC), so they organized 12 teams of four men to match the PSC force. Each team was assigned an M-60 machinegun, four Galil rifles (caliber 5.56), plastic explosives, one sniper rifle, two M79 grenade launchers, four Browning pistols and ammunition. With their training, Kapunan and Rivera figured that the ratio would be 15 to 1 in favor of the rebel camp.

At that time the total strength of the Defense Ministry security force was only 320 officers and men, including Colonel Gador's Cagayan 100, plus 12 teams from the RAM civilian component, which acted as spotters outside the camp. However, the Aguinaldo defenders were highly mobile and were armed with a variety of assault weapons, not to mention their superior training.

The contingency plan was to extricate Enrile and Ramos from Camp Aguinaldo in a bullet-proof van, to be escorted by six 6 × 6 Army trucks and three bullet-proof cars. Two routes were chosen as exit points from Camp Aguinaldo: via the Logistics Command gate at the back of the ministry building or via Gate 1 on Santolan road, depending on the situation.

From Camp Aguinaldo, Enrile and Ramos would transfer to a car at the vicinity of the Labor Hospital on Katipunan road, a kilometer from the camp, and be taken to the RAM base in Bataan, escorted by six of the 12 civilian component teams. Meanwhile, the Reformist troops would engage the loyalists in a delaying action in and around the vicinity of the camp, while awaiting reinforcements.

Kapunan and Rivera estimated that the other RAM contingents at Fort Bonifacio led by Brig. Gen. Rodolfo Canieso, at Villamor Air Base headed by Capt. Fernando Manalo with reinforcements from the PC Training Command under Colonel Fabic, and the Navy headquarters troops of Captain Maligalig should be able to react and reinforce the Crame contingent before daybreak the following day.

Another support unit, the 200-man Special Action Force (SAF) was to split into two groups, with one led by Lt. Col. Rey Velasco, the SAF commander joining Enrile and Ramos in Bataan. The other group would link up with Colonel Honasan and his remaining forces at a rendezvous point in Metro Manila from where they would launch a surprise attack on Malacañang. Honasan would attack the Palace via the Pasig River aboard two hijacked patrol craft fast (PCF) with the help of RAM men in the Navy. Alternate commanders had been named during the planning to replace key officers who may become casualties.

Honasan had estimated that in the actual fighting, only 30 to 40 per cent of the loyalist troops would engage the Enrile-Ramos forces, considering their lack of moral commitment to fight.

To guard against any possibility of mistaken identities, Kapunan devised a visible countersign for rebel forces. A miniature Philippine Flag patch to change position every day, starting with the sun pointed up. Kapunan had used the patch during their training and had stocked more than 5,000 of them. They would come in handy for the assault on Malacañang.

While Kapunan, Rivera, and the other officers planned the escape route, seven RAM officers, including Col. Jose Almonte, Col. Vic Batac, Navy Capt. Felix Turingan, Navy Capt. Rex Robles, Col. Ramon Martinez and Maj. Noe Wong, discussed in another room a plan to harness the National Unification Movement on the side of the Enrile-Ramos camp. The movement was born a week before the February 7 snap election when RAM launched *Kamalayan '86* (Awareness '86) to help ensure clean, orderly and honest elections. It enlisted the participation of retired generals, who in turn formed their own Senior Cavalier Reform AFP Movement (SCRAM), civic organizations like Lions, Rotary, Kiwanis, Jaycees; religious groups and the business sector.

It was time to contact the leaders of these organizations for support to Enrile and Ramos. And the job was assigned to Col. Cesar Bello and two other RAM officers.

The first to be contacted was Agapito "Butz" Aquino, a brother of the late Sen. Benigno Aquino and head of the August Twenty-One

Movement (ATOM), an umbrella organization for moderate and radical groups protesting the assassination of Senator Aquino.

Butz met Enrile in Camp Aguinaldo. Businessman-activist Jaime Ongpin, Jose Concepcion, and other officers of the National Movement for Free Elections (NAMFREL) were also contacted.

A chain reaction ensued. By 10:30 p.m., as Marcos appeared on TV reacting to the Enrile-Ramos revolt, some 50,000 people gathered around Camp Aguinaldo and formed a human barricade to protect the gutsy duo.

"It was the beginning of people power," observed Emil Ong, a businessman and Aquino supporter. Ong was in his house when he heard Cardinal Sin's appeal to the people over the radio to support Enrile and Ramos and to bring food to the camp. Ong was among the first to respond. He and a friend, Jose Balite, brought six boxes of canned goods for the rebels.

The crowd around the camp increased by the hour but at dusk their numbers had dwindled to less than 3,000. RAM spotters were worried. They warned that unless something was done about the thinning crowd, the camp would become vulnerable to attack.

The seven officers devised a new plan to recall people power to EDSA. A newspaperman present during the strategy meetings suggested the use of media, particularly radio and television.

A quick look at the media structure in Metro Manila and the rest of the country convinced the officers that the plan would work. There were 244 newspapers in the country, 33 of which were based in Metro Manila, including seven big national dailies. There were 185 weekly publications, including 46 comics magazines, circulated mostly in Metro Manila.

Electronics media accounted for 286 radio stations, of which 46 were broadcasting from Metro Manila. There were 26 television stations throughout the country, five of them in the metropolis. The Manila networks had ten relay stations nationwide. The government-owned Voice of the Philippines and the Maharlika Broadcasting System operated 22 radio stations and five TV stations nationwide, respectively.

The newsman reminded the planners that Minister Enrile and General Ramos had the capability to preempt the use of these vast media outlets as a psychological propaganda weapon. Preemptive action would necessarily deny Malacañang maximum access to media, and Marcos would lose the propaganda war.

Enrile lost no time when he was informed of the plan. He ordered his public information assistants, Brig. Gen. Eduardo Ermita, lawyer Jose Flores, Jr., Silvestre Afable, and Col. Luis San Andres, General Ramos' spokesman, to get in touch quietly with their friends in media.

At 6 a.m. (Day 2), Enrile was told the bad news: Radio Veritas had been destroyed. He was worried. His face, however, broke into a wide grin when he was informed that large segments of the print and broadcast media had been disseminating to the nation and to the world the gallant stand at Camp Crame.

Thus, through the magic of mass media, Enrile and Ramos were able to galvanize people power and rally it back to EDSA. But more important, from the strategic military point of view, they were able, through the mass media, to reach out to the ordinary soldiers — they who had their fingers on the trigger — to confirm to them in that precise moment of crisis what they had known all along: That precisely because of the reasons that had been stated, their President and Commander-in-Chief had lost the legal and moral right to lead them, and the nation.

Also because of the media, RAM members in the regional and provincial commands were able to react instantly to the crisis. The time gained from the rapid flow of information made possible the timely activation of previously prepared scenarios designed to prevent loyalist reinforcements from moving to Manila.

One such scenario, code-named "Operation Freeze" and authored by Colonel Honasan, called for the immobilization of loyalist troops in the countryside. It was activated as early as Day 1 of the revolution.

At the RUC 10 Headquarters in Cagayan de Oro, nine RAM officers led by Lt. Col. Tibursio Fusilero and Lt. Col. Art Lumibao staged their own silent and bloodless mutiny on Day 2, which paralyzed the whole command and prevented it from sending troops to Manila.

At RUC 7, the Heavy Airlift Command in Cebu City, which had the planes to transport loyalist forces to Manila, was immobilized as early as before midnight of Saturday, through the clandestine work of two RAM officers, Lt. Col. Joseph Ramos and Lt. Gol. Neon Ebuen. Ground Forces identified with Marcos and Ver in Bohol and adjacent provinces in the RUC area were similary frozen through the underground work of RAM officers Lt. Col. Jose G. Ayap, 2nd Lt. Augusto M. Marquez and 2nd Lt. Eduardo S. Ebon.

At RUC 1, Brig. Gen. Tomas Dumpit, a rabid Ver loyalist, was helpless. His deputy, Col. Manuel Lopez, announced on Day 2 that he had defected to the Enrile-Ramos camp. Others followed: Maj. Jun Jimenez, Dumpit's Air Force component commander; Lt. Col. Flor Fianza, General Ramos' former aide who was on Dumpit's staff; Capt. Bong Ibrado, General Ramas' intelligence officer in the region, Lt. Col. Marciano Ilagan, Camp John Hay base commander, and Lt. Benjie Magalang, commander of the 191st Ranger Company.

Magalang's men provided security for the defecting officers. All the Filipino soldeirs at Camp John Hay also defected and organized themselves into a security force to protect American nationals in the base.

On that day, too, the entire Philippine Military Academy cadet corps of 770 men switched loyalty to Enrile and Ramos through the efforts of Honasan's classmate, Lt. Col. Nelson Eslao, deputy commandant of the Academy. However, the defection was not announced until Day 3 at 1:45 a.m., when all the cadets were armed and ready to move to Camp Crame. Thirty minutes later, the entire cadet corps of the National Police Academy had armed themselves and announced their defection to Enrile and Ramos.

At Regional Unified Command 2, known as Enrile country, the problem was a small one. Officers with the NISA remained loyal to Marcos and Ver, but kept peace with the rebel forces to avoid bloodshed.

The bulk of the 5th Army Division was marooned at Fort Magsaysay in Nueva Ecija. In Pampanga, Lt. Col. Reynaldo Beroya's men put up a secondary blockade, augmented by people power.

In RUC 4, RUC 5, RUC 6, RUC 7, RUC 9, RUC 11, and RUC 12, a similar bloodless mutiny had been staged by RAM officers, in different intervals of time during the four-day revolution, with the support of people power. It is unfortunate, however, that specific details could not be mentioned because by doing so would unnecessarily expose the names of some of the men involved, many of whom are engaged in intelligence operations against communist terrorists and organized crime syndicates.

Because of the confusion on Day 1, many RAM officers were unable to report to their respective units. On Day 2, 46 RAM officers reported to Camp Crame where they helped run the Enrile-Ramos War Room. Among them: Army Col. Ismael "Billy" Villareal, PC Capt. Charlemagne Alejandrino, PC Capt. Rosendo Ferrer, PC Maj. Walter Besas, PC Maj. Servando Hizon, PC Maj. Doroteo Reyes, PC Maj. Samuel Bagasin, Army Maj. Alex Dimabuyo, Army Maj. Delfin Lorenzana. Army Maj. Fernando Patawaran, Comdr. Matthew Mayuga, Comdr. Ephraim Rio, Marine Maj. Emmanuel Teodosio, Air Force Capt. Raul Gonzales, Air Force Capt. Merito Quijano, Air Force Capt. Rene Badilla, Air Force Capt. Rodolfo Petican, Air Force Capt. Meynardo Santiago.

PC Capt. Fernando Mesa, PC Capt. Ray Roderos, Lt. (sg) Reynaldo Ansay, Capt. Teofilo Melliza, Police Maj. John Castro, PC Lt. Col. Dominador Domingo, PC Col. Cesar Nazareno, PC Col. Virgilio David, Army Col. Ray Jarque, PC Col. Bert Rodriguez, PC Col. Plaridel Abaya, PC Maj. Napoleon de los Santos, PC Capt. Francisco Nato, PC Col. Guillermo Domondon, Col. Santiago Aliño, PC Maj. Pete Cadungog, PC Col. Romeo Zulueta, PC Col. Raul Imperial, PC Col. Pat Lomongo, PC Lt. Col. Rex Piad, PC Col. Manuel Bruan, Lt. Col. Francisco, Maj. Osia, and Lt. Sison.

No defense plan for Camp Crame had been mapped out when Ramos returned to the camp after the breakaway announcement at Camp Aguinaldo. Capt. Charlemagne Alejandrino, backed by a handful of lower-ranked officers took charge of the operations. At 4:30 a.m., Sunday, Aguirre arrived from Baguio, but before proceeding to Camp Crame, he passed by Radio Veritas to help belie Marcos' claim of a coup plot hatched by the military. He also left a tape-recorded statement appealing to those "who value truth, justice, fairness, professionalism and real service to the people to support General Ramos and Minister Enrile."

At Camp Crame, Aguirre reported to General Ramos, who gave him instructions: "Set up camp defense, galvanize and make maximum use of people power but undertake no provocative military action against loyalist forces."

Aguirre met with his men and the RAM volunteers. He divided them into two groups, one to stay with him as operations staff, the other led by Majors Reyes and Hizon to stay outside and move around as intelligence operatives. They were also directed to contact their classmates in the Academy and other sympathizers for the Enrile-Ramos cause.

The information gathered by the intelligence operatives enabled Aguirre to block strategic routes to the camp. At that time, no tactical information was being received from regular intelligence sources. However, this was corrected later in the day following a coordinating meeting presided over by Brig. Gen. Jacinto Galang, Constabulary chief of staff.

The Operations Center was not in the same room as the Command Center (War Room), which was situated at Ramos' office some distance away. Initially, this caused some miscoordination, but was remedied immediately after a meeting with Navy Capt. Jesus Durian, who was in charge of the War Room.

An inventory of forces in Camp Crame showed that the rebel side was inferior in strength, in terms of number and firepower. The camp had the headquarters company and the Headquarters Service Battalion contingency force (a battalion minus) under Col. Paterno Lomongo, two Special Action Force companies under Lt. Col. Rey Velasco, a company-minus from the training command under Lt. Col. Hercules Cataluña and the office personnel of various units, who had been issued firearms.

When Enrile marched to Camp Crame to join Ramos at 2:24 p.m. that Sunday, the camp had only 450 officers and men, augmented by Enrile's own force of 320 men, including Gador's Cagayan 100.

Colonel Villareal's familiarity with the capability, strength, and identities of units loyal to Marcos and Ver, which he acquired during his long tenure as AFP operations branch chief at general headquarters, came in handy throughout the crisis. Villareal also had maintained contact with mass organizers for the Corazon Aquino for President Movement (CAPM). Through these organizing officers, the War Room was able to mobilize, shift or organize people's barricades at threatened approaches to the camp.

Among these organizing officers are lawyer Amor Reyes, Roberto Gabuna, Grace Veloso Bucu, Robert Bucu III, Joey Ibay, Tony Villaruz Selda, Casey Alejandre, Roger Cleofe, Pepe Neyra, Jules de Vera, Manny Roxas, Tony Molina, Silverio Florentin, Dr. Geronimo Lavilla, Benny de Ocampo, Gener Sula, Peter Tan, Adonis Quianan, Fernando Totoy Velasquez and Leonardo Bonayon. Tan's communication system in Eagle Communications, and the communication systems of the Kiwanis Club of Manila North and the Kiwanis Club of Kalayaan, Quezon City, helped the organizers monitor the movement of loyalist troops towards Camp Crame.

Two RAM officers, Lt. Col. Ruben Gange and Lt. Col. Ceferino Sarmenta, Jr., who resigned from the service to dramatize their hatred of the Marcos-Ver clique, were among the first to join Enrile and Ramos. They coordinated with their classmate, Lt. Col. Rolando Garcia, in gathering intelligence information.

Lt. Col. Rodolfo Vasquez, another Reformist officer, and Simon "Toto" Samonte, Mrs. Enrile's aide, were not in the camp during the four-day revolution but they had a job that was just as dangerous and as important. Their assignment was to secure Cristina, the minister's wife, their children and grandchildren.

To avoid danger, Vasquez and Samonte transferred the minister's family from one friend's house to another.

Even in the United States where mutiny could mean incarceration, seven Reformist officers studying at the US Army school in Fort Lee, Virginia, motored to Washington, D.C., occupied the Philippine embassy and declared they were supporting the revolt.

The officers, later commended by Enrile and Ramos, were Army Lt. Col. Arturo B. Carillo, Army Capt. Joseph Li, Army Capt. Arturo Querol, Army Capt. Arnold Pangilinan, PC Capt. Jun Manga, PC Capt. Artemio Rodriguez and PC Capt. Winifredo Borja.

Another Reformist, Col. Hernani Figueroa, an intelligence and psywar expert, was given another job — and almost paid for it with his life. His mission was to divert the attention of Ver and his agents from RAM's inner core. To accomplish the mission, Figueroa devised his own strategy: He launched a one-man war against Ver and company. Making full use of the media, he denounced the general and his clique in the armed forces at every turn, blaming them for the corruption and the demoralization in the ranks of the military.

Figueroa's campaign against Ver was so effective that in time, the general's men were concentrating their attention on this seemingly brash RAM officer, and all but ignored the activities of the other members.

On Day 3 of the Revolution, Figueroa saw how close he had come to courting death at the hands of Ver's henchmen. He had been holed up with General Ramos at Camp Crame since Day 1, but on Monday, Figueroa slipped out of camp to visit his wife and children in their quarters at Camp Aguinaldo. Soon after he cleared the gate, a group of armed loyalists was on his tail. They followed him to his quarters. He knew he would be arrested, and perhaps silenced forever.

Figueroa realized that the loyalists were waiting for him outside his quarters as he was changing to more comfortable clothing. He decided to escape before they could surround the house. He jumped out of a window near the kitchen and ran to a nearby cottage, occupied by a military chaplain, little realizing that he was in his underwear.

A garbage truck was parked outside the chaplain's cottage. Figueroa climbed into the truck and hid under a pile of dried leaves.

He stayed there until the truck moved out of the camp. As it inched its way through the multitude, Figueroa jumped out of the truck. To conceal his embarrassment, he started jumping up and down like crazy, pretending lunacy, until he got to a telephone. He asked his wife to bring him decent clothing. "I was lucky nobody recognized me," he told Minister Enrile after the revolution.

The rest of the exploits of the RAM are written in the pages of the history of the revolution elsewhere in this book. It is a story of courage and heroism, but above all, of patriotism. And as the nation proceeds to bind the wounds of that conflict, and as it continues to build a just and democratic society under God, it is assured that the leadership of its Armed Forces will remain in the hands of reform-minded and selfless officers like the members of the RAM.

For the RAM, by its participation in the revolution, has institutionalized a covenant with the people. Forged on the anvil at EDSA, it is a covenant that is both an article of faith and a warning to would-be-tyrants — that never again shall the liberty of the nation be compromised in the interest of one man. □

PICTORIAL

△ *The historic moment: Defense Minister Juan Ponce Enrile (right) and Vice Chief of Staff Lt. Gen. Fidel V. Ramos, announce the withdrawal of their support from the Marcos government.*

△ *This helicopter sneaked out of Villamor Air Base to bring arms and ammunition for the "Cagayan 100" contingent that secretly made its way to Camp Aguinaldo.*

Soldiers of the "Cagayan 100" contingent take their weapons from the helicopter. It was another aircraft, the minister's "Cristina," that brought in the arms from Cagayan and temporarily cached them at Villamor Air Base.

△   Rebel troops get the feel of their guns and survey their field of fire
       as they assume defensive positions at the ministry building.

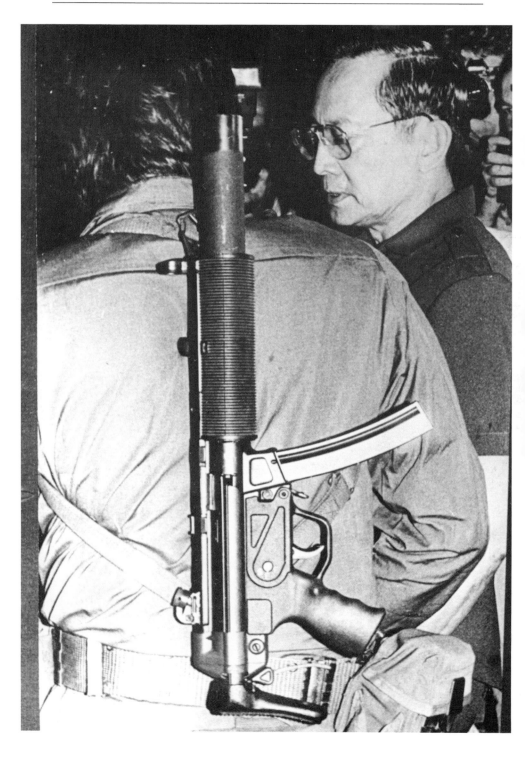

△ *Two of the key officers of the Reform the Armed Forces Movement, Maj. Noe Wong and Col. Gregorio Honasan point to the author, at right, in a map various locations of General Ver's safehouses in Metro Manila prior to the revolution.*

◁ *The two revolutionary leaders in close consultation.*

Reformist officers with Philippine flag patches talk to Marine soldiers at Camp Aguinaldo on Day 3, to join the Enrile-Ramos camp.

△   *Response to Radio Veritas' appeal to the public to donate food for
the rebels was immediate.*

△   *Rebel soldier receiving Holy Communion from a Catholic priest.*

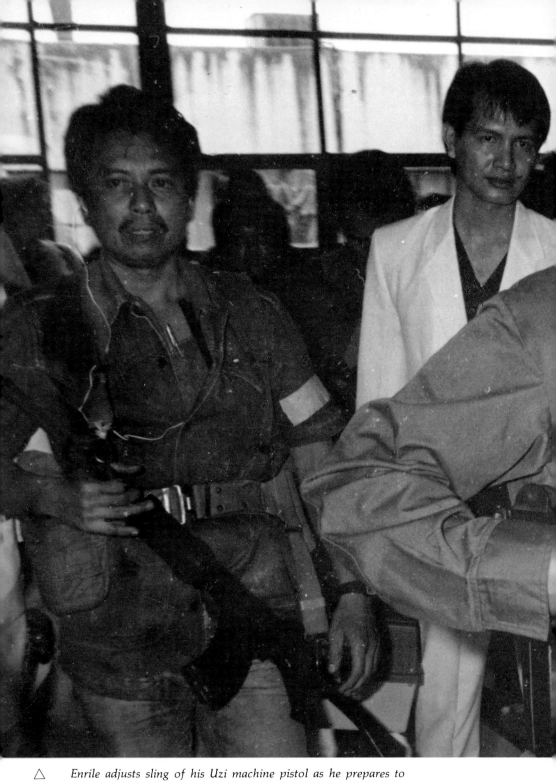

△ *Enrile adjusts sling of his Uzi machine pistol as he prepares to vacate his office to join Ramos at Camp Crame.*

△ *Enrile flashing the "laban sign."*

 Enrile moved from Camp Aguinaldo to Camp Crame and joined Ramos for a tighter defense position.

△ *Howitzers positioned at Camp Aguinaldo on Day 3 for a barrage*
   that would reduce the rebel headquarters into debris. They were
   never fired.

△　*Marcos troops going on foot to designated attack position are blocked by human barricades.*

△ *Lt. Col. Jake Malajacan, Major Saulito Aromin and Major Ricardo Brillantes, three of the four officers presented at a press conference by Marcos as participants in the "plot" to assassinate him and Mrs. Marcos. The other officer was Capt. Morales, an escort officer of Mrs. Marcos.*

△ People stall a convoy of Marcos crowd control troops on their way to assist the Marines.

▽ Marines relax while waiting for the result of negotiations between their officers and people's power leaders, and orders from Fort Bonifacio.

In Quezon City, during the battle for the broadcasting stations, a man with rosary beads stands in the path of an armored vehicle carrying reinforcing Marcos troops.

△   *Armored tip of juggernaut sent to crush Enrile, Ramos, and Reformist rebels.*

△ Armored personnel carrier of Marcos loyalists went through a cement wall after by-passing a human barricade at the Corinthian Gardens.

▽ Armor is stopped by a sea of humanity in its path. (It is not these few hands that did it; it's the massive human obstacle.)

△ *Armored vehicles maneuver to turn back after the attack was called off.*

▽ *Aerial view of Channel 4 TV station.*

△ *Attack column spearheaded by armor rolls toward Camp Crame on EDSA.*

△   *Enrile shaking hands with Tañada, while Ongpin, center, watches.*

▽   *Enrile and Ramos with Tingting Cojuangco.*

Reformist soldier is the teenagers' new model for the "macho" man.

△ *Reformist soldier stands guard atop a helicopter that flew into Camp Crame to be in the service of Enrile and Ramos.*

△   *This is the main gate of Camp Crame, bastion of the revolution,*
    with its human "security blanket."

△ *Reformist troops guard the approaches to the MND Building.*

△   *Mortar crew with their weapon ready to fire on Camp Crame on Day 3.*

△ Defiant and self-confident, Marcos speaks at a televised press conference to show that the armed forces is still loyal to him.

△ *Marcos shows the four Reformist officers to his left, who were arrested for allegedly having plotted to assassinate him and his wife.*

△ *Ver insists on "annihilating" the rebels but Marcos advices him not to fire. Never-*
theless, on Marcos' orders the troops were on their way to attack Camp Crame.

△ *Smoke billows from a helicopter hit by rebel raiders. All the target choppers were
destroyed, one completely. The fixed-wing craft at right were intentionally spared.*

△ *A firefighter desperately fights the flames eating up a helicopter hit in a raid by rebel pilots.*

▽ *Crowds swarm around one of the helicopters that went over to the rebel side.*

△ *Under orders to hit Camp Crame, helicopters of the 15th Strike Wing land at the Camp instead and defect to the rebel side. The crowd is jubilant over the incident.*

△   Enrile and Ramos in prayer.

△ *After the capture of a station by rebels, people barricade the area as insurance against counter-attack.*

▽ *Rally at the main gate of Camp Crame. Enrile, Ramos beside him, waves at cheering crowd.*

△ *Enrile speaks before the crowd at the Constabulary headquarters building. Ramos is to his right. Priest is Fr. Bert Clemeña who was mauled in Legaspi City by Marcos partisans during the elections.*

△   *Enrile and Ramos see victory in sight on the last day of the revolution. They encourage the crowd with their estimate of the situation.*

△ *Minister Enrile meets the press after the collapse of the Marcos regime. Note shoulder patch, upside down flag, indicating third day of the revolution.*

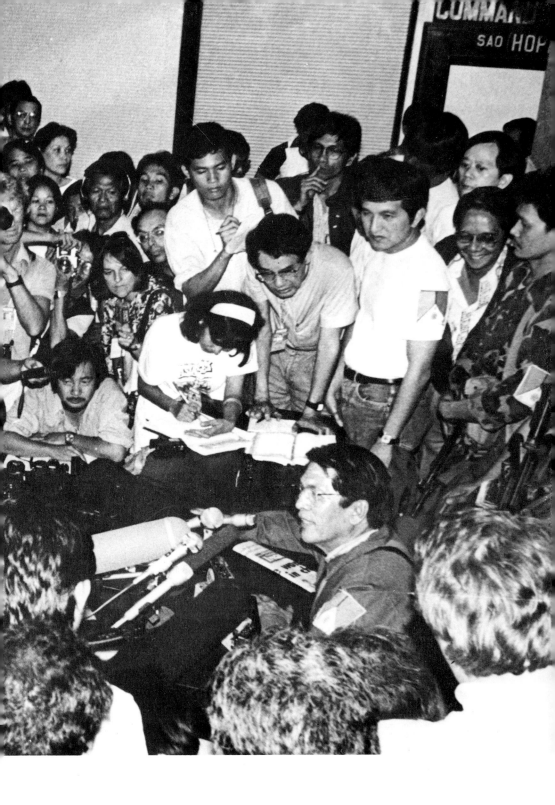

△ *Marcos delivers his inaugural address. His oath of office as president had just been administered by Chief Justice Ramon C. Aquino (in dark suit). Mrs. Marcos stands sullenly by.*

△ *From Palace balcony, Marcos waves to the crowd below. Mrs. Marcos tries to smile.*

△ *Marcos daughters, Imee M. Manotoc and Irene M. Araneta. Tall man at right is*
   Tommy Manotoc, Imee's husband. For the ladies, like mother, no expensive jewelry.

Mrs. Marcos stands, suppressing tears, behind her husband as he delivers his inaugural address. She wears none of her fabulous diamond rings. Not even her wedding rings. Son, Gov. Ferdinand Marcos II, in fatigue uniform, looks dazed.

△ *Portion of the crowd of Marcos followers that came into the Palace grounds to see the inauguration ceremonies.*

▽ *Flag-waving people at the Malacañang grounds during the inaugural of Marcos.*

△ *In better times, Mrs. Marcos would be at her smiling and triumphant best. But it looks like she's rehearsing, "Parting is such sweet sorrow."*

△ *Flimsy wall of stone-filled bags is laid across EDSA as the people move toward Ortigas to firm up the human barricades there.*

△ *Ver's reinforcements in an armored vehicle are persuaded by
   people to go back.*

Capt. Phil Plaza in firefight during the skirmish for possession of Channel 9 studios.
The officer came out of it slightly wounded.

Task Force Delta troopers were augmented by soldiers from
Camp Crame. These are the reinforcement.

Defense Minister Juan Ponce Enrile, left, gives President Corazon C. Aquino her first cabinet briefing on the overall situation on Day 4 at a secret place in Wack-Wack, Mandaluyong, Metro Manila, a few hours after she took oath of office as President.

△ *Newsmen hit the dirt as the firefight rages at Channel 9.*

Casualty in Marcos' army is lowered from the television tower
after rebel troops captured Channel 9.

△ *The battle for the airlanes was won on the very first day by the Reformists. Here a soldier guarding a broadcasting station is alerted at the slightest sign of trouble.*

▽ *This is one of the armories of the elite security forces of Marcos which was captured intact by rebel forces outside of Metro Manila on Day 4 of the revolution. Among the armaments shown in the picture are M-60 machineguns, M-14 rifles, Israeli-made Galil rifles, 9mm Uzi machine pistols, plastic explosives and boxes of assorted ammo.*

△ *Thousands of Aquino partisans outside Malacañang waiting for the opportune time to crash through the gates when it was known that the Marcoses were leaving. Marcos partisans, outnumbered, simply evaporated.*

▽ *People clamber up the iron fence of Malacañang after it was known that the Marcoses had flown to Clark. The Palace was looted.*

△ *Aquino partisans who invaded Malacañang on Day 4 carry away a mutilated can-*
   vass with a portrait of Mrs. Marcos.

△ Human barricades at the main gate of Camp Crame. They are cheering Enrile and
Ramos who appeared on an improvised stage to speak to them.

△ *At the people's barricades on EDSA, the night is spent by religious groups on prayer and this consists of interminable rosaries.*

▽ *View of "people power" from Camps Crame and Aguinaldo to infinity in the direction of Ortigas Avenue. The assault force, if it could afford to do it, would have to plow through this human sea.*

△   *From the fertile minds of the impetuous youth come variety of slogans like this one.*

▽   *School girls plead with soldiers of Marcos' army not to go any further.*

△ *This is people versus armor. The people refuse to be terrorized and the armor left them alone.*

△ *People burn the portrait of Marcos*

△ Reformist officers in an out-of-town jaunt to keep themselves in a high state of proficiency in fighting under any environment. At left, above, is Col. "Gringo" Honasan and Col. Red Kapunan. At left, below, is Col. Rey Rivera and Col. Tito Legaspi.

△ *Enrile with his machine pistol.*

△   *These Reformist officers are target practicing in one of their*
    indoor trainings in Quezon province.

△ *This is one of the training exercises of the Reformist officers in the Cordilleras, recorded by the author with his camera before the revolution. This photo shows a 7-man team boarding a helicopter after a mock assault on an enemy territory.*

△ *These are the Reformist officers behind plans for tactical moves of participating units defending Camps Aguinaldo and Crame during the revolution. They constituted the close-in security of Minister Enrile. Head of the group is Col. Gregorio "Gringo" Honasan (standing, in camouflage uniform).*

An estimated million attended Holy Mass celebrated by Jaime
Cardinal Sin at the Rizal Park in Manila after the revolution.

REFERENCES

Notes on: Exclusive interview with Defense Minister Juan Ponce Enrile in his residence and office on February 27, 29 and March 2, 4, 7, 8 and 17.

NARRATIVE REPORTS (Declassified):

1. Maj. Gen. Vicente Piccio, Jr.
   Commanding General
   Philippine Air Force

2. Brig. Gen. Artemio Tadiar, Jr.
   Commandant
   Philippine Marines

3. Brig. Gen. Felix Brawner, Jr.
   Commanding General
   First Scout Ranger Regiment

4. Brig. Gen. Andres Ramos
   Commanding General
   Regional Unified Command IV

5. Brig. Gen. Isidoro de Guzman
   Commanding General
   5th Infantry Division
   Philippine Army

6. Brig. Gen. Antonio Palafox
   Commanding General
   5th Infantry Division
   Philippine Army

7. Brig. Gen. Jose Ma. Carlos
   Zumel
   Superintendent
   Philippine Military Academy

8. Brig. Gen. Godofredo Sta. Ana
   Commanding General
   3rd Air Division
   Philippine Air Force

9. Commodore Liberato L. Lazo
   Commandant
   Philippine Coast Guard

10. Brig. Gen. Pedro Balbanero
    Commanding General
    Military Police Brigade

11. Col. Braulio Balbas
    Deputy Commandant
    Philippine Marines

12. Col. Galileo Kintanar
    Deputy Chief
    Intelligence Service, AFP

13. Col. Alexander Aguirre
    Chief of Operations
    Headquarters, Philippine
    Constabulary

14. Col. Emiliano D. Templo
    Chief of Staff
    PC Metropolitan Command

15. Col. Alexander Galido
    Commanding Officer, 3rd
    Brigade, 2nd Infantry Division
    Philippine Army

16. Col. Dioscoro E. Yoro, Jr.
    Deputy Commander
    Civil Relations Service, AFP

17. Col. Antonio Sotelo
    Commanding Officer
    15th Strike Wing
    Philippine Air Force

18. Col. Rogelio E. Luis
    National Intelligence and
    Security Authority

19. Capt. (PN) Eriberto Varona
    Secretary, General Staff

20. Col. Vicente B. Tigas
    Media Officer
    Presidential Security Command

21. Col. Balbino Diego
    Chief Legal Officer
    Presidential Security Command

22. Lt. Col. Cesar I. Alvarez
    Provincial Commander
    Bulacan Constabulary Command

23. Lt. Col. Eduardo S. Matillano
    Commander
    Task Force "Delta"

AFTER OPERATIONS REPORT
(Declassified):

1. Brig. Gen. Benjamin Divinagracia
   Commanding General
   3rd Infantry (Spearhead) Division
   Philippine Army

2. Police Brig. Gen. Alfredo S. Lim
   Superintendent
   Northern Police District

3. Col. Roger E. Deinla
   Deputy Task Force Commander
   PC Regional Command VII

TRANSCRIPTS OF PRESS
CONFERENCES WITH MINISTER
ENRILE AND GENERAL RAMOS:

1. February 22, 1986

2. February 23, 1986

3. February 24, 1986

4. February 25, 1986

5. February 26, 1986

6. February 27, 1986

LETTERS TO THE AFP CHIEF OF ·
STAFF:

1. Maj. Gen. Josephus Q. Ramas
   Commanding General
   Philippine Army

2. Maj. Gen. Prospero Olivas
   Commanding General
   PC Metropolitan Command

MEMORANDUM FOR:

1. Gen. Fidel V. Ramos
   Chief of Staff, New Armed Forces
   of the Philippines, from Brig.
   Gen. Santiago Barangan

REPORTS FROM ABROAD
SUBMITTED TO MINISTER
ENRILE:

1. Embassy of the Philippines
   Washington, D.C.

2. Philippine Consulate
   Los Angeles, California, USA

3. Captain Carlos I. Agustin
   Defense Attache, Embassy of the
      Philippines, Washington, D.C.
   (On Activities During the
      February Revolution)

BATASANG PAMBANSA
(PARLIAMENT) RECORDS:

1. The Electoral Tribunal
2. Tally Report
3. Proclamation

LOGBOOKS (Classified):

1. Passenger Manifest on US
   Aircraft Bearing FM and Party

2. Cargo Manifest

DECREE:

1. Presidential Decree No. 731
   (On Succession)

LETTER OF INSTRUCTIONS:

1. Letter of Instructions 776
   (Relief, reassignment and
      promotion of military officers)

INTELLIGENCE JOURNALS
(Classified):

1. C-3 Division
2. J-2 Tactical Operations Center
3. Intelligence Service, AFP
   Tactical Operations Center
4. Press Center, Office of Media
   Affairs,
   Office of the President

INTELLIGENCE REPORTS
(Classified) SUBMITTED TO
MINISTER ENRILE:

1. *Reform the Armed Forces
   Movement (RAM)*
2. *Recorded Actions of General Ver
   from 21 February to 25
   February, 1986, gathered through
   Radio Intercepts and Intelligence
   Operations*

INTERNAL PUBLICATIONS:

*A Brief Account of the People's
   Revolution
   (Chief Record Division, OJ3, New
   AFP)*

*Accounts of Incidents, Joint
   Operations Center Journal*

*Philippine Army Operations
   Center Journal*

*Philippine Constabulary Operations
   Center Journal*

*Philippine Air Force Operations
   Center Journal*

Navy Operations Center Journal

INDEX

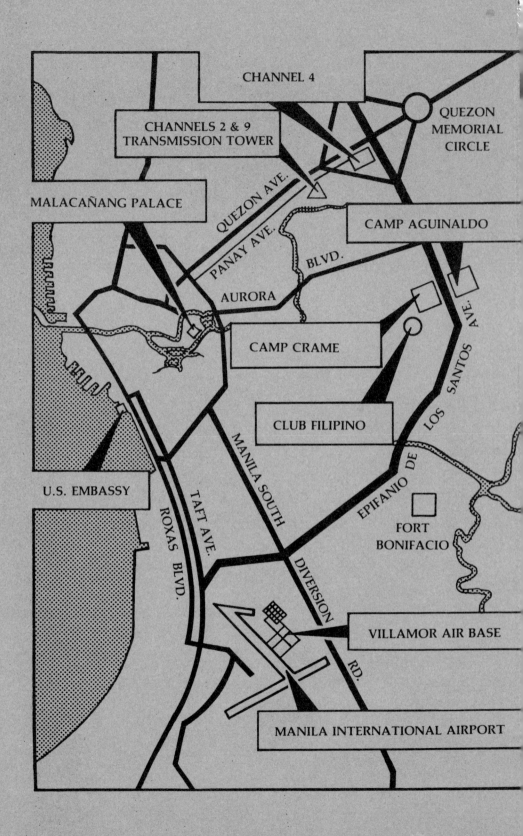